"In this beautiful and shimmering volume we encounter Mike Eigen, the ultimate psychoanalytic alchemist creating an expansive healing brew of psychoanalysis, mysticism and plain common sense. From the Bal Shem Tov to Bion, From Winnicott to Whitman; from a half filled cup of coffee that causes a psychic catastrophe to the dream of a patient's arm falling off that opens up infinities, Eigen takes us into the depths and vastness of what it means to be human, and teaches us the wisdom of our patients' symptoms and the pain, joy and strain of staying close to their deep suffering and struggle. Eigen's alchemy not only transforms the practice of psychotherapy, but transforms one's sense of life itself. Keep this book close at hand, dip into it often and read it again and again."

Robert Grossmark, Ph.D, ABPP, New York University Postdoctoral Program in Psychoanalysis and Psychotherapy, author of *The Unobtrusive Relational Analyst: Explorations in Psychoanalytic Companioning*, co-editor of *The One and The Many: Relational Approaches to Group Psychotherapy* and *Heterosexual Masculinities: Perspectives from Psychoanalytic Gender Theory*

"Is it an inherent part of being a psychoanalyst that one is also wise? My first contact with the work of Eigen confirmed that he was wise, but there was some caution in my psychoanalytic group about his work – was it 'wild' – was it 'spiritual' – was it not 'psychoanalysis'. Like Bion he is intrepid in the psychic hell holes he will enter, and also like Bion appreciates beauty at the same time. Reading this book he is undoubtably a psychoanalyst – and a wise, compassionate, one at that."

Nicola Abel-Hirsch, author of *Bion: 365 Quotes*, Training Analyst British Psychoanalytic Society

"Michael Eigen gives us a poetic space where psychoanalysis, radical ethics and the holy live together. This book provides a stunning lens into his earlier work while always stretching us to see and hear more. A perfect companion in our world of plague."

Donna M. Orange, author of *Psychoanalysis, History, and Radical Ethics: Learning to Hear*

"*Eigen in Seoul* is soul in Seoul. The book spans the third Seoul seminar given by Eigen over a three-day period, but I read it, intrigued, in one sitting. Written in Eigen's unique, engaging mode of expression, combining both simplicity and depth. This volume is a fascinating work on aliveness and destruction, openness, freedom and terror, wonder and suffering, helplessness and transformative meeting. It weaves Kabbala, Biblical stories, and therapeutic illustrations, especially Eigen's and Bion's, into our psychic experience, dreaming, and clinical work, enabling deeper contact of being with oneself and others. It brings to mind the Talmudist Ruth Calderon's words: 'There's a belief that the text is waiting for you personally and that God hid a little note with your name on it in the text.' I found immediately the little note with my name in the text. I believe that many readers will find theirs too."

Ofra Eshel, faculty, training and supervising analyst, Israel Psychoanalytic Society, head of Independent Psychoanalysis – Radical Breakthroughs postgraduate track, Tel-Aviv University, author of *The Emergence of Analytic Oneness: Into the Heart of Psychoanalysis*

Eigen in Seoul Volume Three

Between 2007 and 2011, Michael Eigen gave three seminars in Seoul, each running over three days and covering different aspects of psychoanalysis, spirituality and the human psyche. This book is based on a transcription of the third seminar, which took place in 2011, on the subject of Pain and Beauty. The first two were published as *Madness and Murder* (2010) and *Faith and Transformation* (2011).

A conjunction of the pain that shatters and beauty that heals is made by many authors, including Bion, Winnicott, Milner, Meltzer, Perls, Ehrenzweig, Matte-Blanco, Schneur Zalman, Chuang-Tzu, Buber, Castaneda, and Levinas. These and others are used as windows of the psyche, adding to possibilities of experience and opening dimensions that bring us life. Eigen explores challenges of the human psyche, what we are up against and the resources difficulties can stimulate.

This work spans many dimensions of human experience with interplay, fusions and oppositions of pain, beauty, terror, and wonder, and makes use of poetic and philosophical expressions of experience. It will be vital reading for psychoanalysts, psychotherapists, and all those with an interest in psychoanalytic and spiritual psychology.

Michael Eigen teaches at the New York University Postdoctoral Program in Psychotherapy and Psychoanalysis, and the National Psychological Association for Psychoanalysis. He is the author of thirty books and gives a weekly seminar on Bion, Winnicott, Lacan, and his own work, ongoing for nearly fifty years.

Eigen in Seoul Volume Three

Pain and Beauty, Terror and Wonder

Michael Eigen

LONDON AND NEW YORK

First published 2021
by Routledge
2 Park Square, Milton Park, Abingdon, Oxon OX14 4RN

and by Routledge
605 Third Avenue, New York, NY 10158

Routledge is an imprint of the Taylor & Francis Group, an informa business

© 2021 Michael Eigen

The right of Michael Eigen to be identified as author of this work has been asserted by him in accordance with sections 77 and 78 of the Copyright, Designs and Patents Act 1988.

All rights reserved. No part of this book may be reprinted or reproduced or utilised in any form or by any electronic, mechanical, or other means, now known or hereafter invented, including photocopying and recording, or in any information storage or retrieval system, without permission in writing from the publishers.

Trademark notice: Product or corporate names may be trademarks or registered trademarks, and are used only for identification and explanation without intent to infringe.

British Library Cataloguing-in-Publication Data
A catalogue record for this book is available from the British Library

Library of Congress Cataloging-in-Publication Data
A catalog record has been requested for this book

ISBN: 978-1-032-00662-8 (hbk)
ISBN: 978-0-367-75784-7 (pbk)
ISBN: 978-1-003-17510-0 (ebk)

Typeset in Times New Roman
by codeMantra

Contents

Foreword ix
MICHAEL EIGEN

Preface xi
BURTON N SEITLER

Introduction 1
KERI COHEN

1 Day 1   4

2 Day 2   40

3 Day 3   66

References   89
Index   91

Foreword
Michael Eigen

This book is based on a transcription of the third seminar I gave in Seoul in 2011. The first two, given in 2007 and 2009, have already been published as *Madness and Murder* (2010) and *Faith and Transformation* (2011a). I am very thankful to Dr. Jae Hoon Lee for giving me the chance to have the experiences I did. My colleagues in the Seoul Object Relations Institute were welcoming, searching, and simpatico. Each trip has been enriching and deeply moving. I am grateful to Dr. Joon Ho Lee for mediating many of the details, translating my English into Korean, and helping to make the seminar run smoothly. Each seminar was three full days, including morning and afternoon sessions, as you will see. After the last seminar was over, I went to Busan to speak at the First World Humanities Forum (Eigen, 2014a). At my age, approaching mid-eighties, it is not likely that such a long trip will be practical, so I am extra glad I could do it when I did – many good memories.

I also wish to thank my colleague, Keri Cohen, who prodded me to work with the transcriptions and turn them into a book. I delayed doing that for nearly eight years, immersed in many projects and obligations. Keri read the transcriptions and encouraged me to put them into publishable form and contributed elbow grease herself, helping with the editing. I asked her to write an introduction to this work and am glad she said yes.

My work in general spans many dimensions of human experience, perhaps with an interplay of interactions, fusions, oppositions of pain, and beauty. So much of psychoanalysis charts what we do in response to pain. And, as we will see, beauty is the heart of the Kabbalah Tree of Life. Bion wonders how much intensity we can take. So often, it is too much for us, and we try to get rid of it in destructive ways, leading to more pain. Here is simply part of one sentence from Bion's explorations: "How does a person know of pain so impalpable that its intensity, pure intensity, is so intense that it cannot be tolerated but be destroyed even if it involves the murder of the 'anatomical' individual?" (Bion, 1991). Here, Bion links unbearable pain with suicide and murder. One may destroy in order to destroy pain one cannot support.

On the other hand and at the same time, Bion speaks of the beauty of psychoanalysis developing resources for dealing with madness and emotional difficulties, the beauty of learning to help. Kabbalah also writes of brokenness and the ways we work with it, not only to repair (that in itself is a lifelong calling) but to open creative dimensions of experiencing. Various tillers of the psyche will be part of our quest, including Bion, Winnicott, Milner, Meltzer, Elkin, Perls, Ehrenzweig, Matte-Blanco, Green, and Gurwitsch. And many tillers of the spirit, including Schneur Zalman, Chuang-Tzu, Buber, Bohm, Castaneda, Levinas, Akiva, Shimon bar Yochai, Moshe de Leon, and Isaac Luria. Ways in which people are concerned with psychical and spiritual realities not only intersect but interweave in complex, rewarding ways, adding to possibilities of experience and opening dimensions that bring us life.

Preface
Burton N Seitler

After eight years, Michael Eigen has given us a real treat once again. Dr. Eigen compiled – and put into book form – the transcriptions of his third scholarly Seminar in Seoul. Each seminar session was three days in length. His first two sessions dealt with *Madness and Murder*, and *Faith and Transformation*. The third, which is the title of this book, was *Pain and Beauty, Terror and Wonder, Emotional Complexities*.

Ever the wordsmith, Dr. Eigen regales us with his love of and attention to words – their sounds, their multiple levels of meaning; his respect for the manner in which they reveal how one's cultural heritage, phenomenological experiences, and uniquely individual perceptual interpretations can effect personality organization. It is obvious from the start that Eigen derives great joy from his appreciation – almost awe – of the word, its derivations and his multiplicity of associations to it. Even the material from which Eigen quotes makes this point about how words convey many levels and dimensions of meaning. This is amply illustrated by numerous references to Bion, who spoke of "breakdown, breakup, and breakthrough"; Lacan and his emphasis on how the unconscious is structured by (its own) language; and Winnicott's focus on and use of particular words.

Dr. Eigen's chapters include "Bumping into Oneself," feeling "Helpless Against Helplessness," "Heart, Soul and Might," "Hidden Sparks," the "Miracles of Everyday," and "Gestation Beyond Symptoms." All contain vignettes of Eigen's patients' exquisitely painful feelings – sometimes expressed indirectly, obliquely, or even without words. Here, we bear witness to Eigen as psychoanalytic artist, not fully knowing when and when not to speak but nonetheless constructing ways to communicate with the person in need in some fashion, creating an empathic bond and knowing (perhaps not knowing but feeling) what the person is trying to say and what they want. He speaks of a "rhythm of faith," which includes the whole sequence of a person's agony, dying to oneself and rebirth, and coming alive again. Here too, Eigen has faith in the process of being with rather than talking "at."

If you are interested in a very original synthesis of philosophy, philology, and psychoanalytic perspectives, then this is the book for you. It is at once a blend of scholarly ideas without being tedious or boring, along with creative originality without being wild-eyed or all over the place. But this is much more than a theoretical, high-minded, abstract treatise – although there are also embedded theoretical conceptualizations sufficient to satisfy one's intellectual appetite.

However, of even greater importance, this is a very real, down-to-earth, practical book, which details the raw anguish, deep throbbing cuts, and personal stories of human beings like you and me in the throes of horrible, unrelenting pain. Warning: this book is not for the faint of heart. It underscores the fact that this work requires total immersion, investment, commitment, dedication, and a dogged refusal to give up, the kind of attributes that Eigen has exemplified over several decades.

Read it. You just might acquire sufficient serenity from Eigen's close encounters with the most primitive parts of the unconscious and gain just enough to be able to be of help by bearing witness to the face of abject terror that persons exhibiting psychotic experiences expose us to (undoubtedly what they themselves may have been traumatized by).

—Burton N. Seitler, PhD, Editor, *JASPER*; 2019
NAAP Gradiva Award winner

Introduction
Keri Cohen

In this third volume of Michael Eigen's Seoul seminars, Eigen takes us out of our psyches and into the Universe, as he continues to enlarge the field. What does this mean? Eigen's ability to help us see the beauty and terror of the world both inside and beyond our own psyches helps us expand capacities of function. He teaches us to value our psyche in relation to all of its parts. Our psyche is bigger than any one part, any one experience, any one hurt, any one failure. He urges us to widen the field of vision to include multitudes. Like Bion, he values the periphery vision. I think of the word "timelessness" and wish there was a word for "infinite psyche." Eigen very much teaches us to think in terms of the Universe, like the Universe can contain us, anything, our psyches. The Universe is inside of us.

Eigen beautifully shows us time and time again, simplistic beauty nestled in the complex matrix of the terror in our beings. He calls for us to excavate this area, like an archaeological dig.

In parts of this volume Eigen walks us through his midrash of his own works, including *Feeling Matters* and *Flames from the Unconscious*. He takes us through dreams, teaching how he feels and thinks about the dream process. Eigen revisits the connection between Kabbalah and Psychoanalysis, expanding upon his earlier work. Through revisiting of some of his work, he oscillates between then and now, introducing us to his inner architecture or blueprints of his work. He shares the deeper how and what of his psychic process.

New ways to pay attention to patients' inner lives through the Question and Answer sessions with the audience are discovered. Advocating for every tiny morsel of strength one contains, Eigen encourages patients and us all to make use of what is possible, even if only a tiny spark. The belief that "every little bit" counts proves to be essential. He manufactures psychic oxygen in an effort to help us breathe. His work serves as an incubator for our embryonic parts.

Eigen muses that because this is his third time in Seoul, that there is nothing new he could possibly say, but as one absorbs the thoughts and feelings radiating in the pages of this volume, one begins to understand the timelessness of the infinite psyche, of Eigen's infinite psyche and how it operates. He pays homage to the conflicting parts within the psyche, exercising it as a fluid, living, growing organ.

Day 1 teaches the audience the importance of walking around oneself, one's psyche, as opposed to "bumping into oneself." Bumping into oneself becomes informative as well. Without it one may not begin to take in the value of walking around the obstacle we sometimes call our mind. Eigen emphasizes the importance of not thinking so much as feeling one's way into waiting, being able to wait. The emphasis is on creating a gap or caesura between impulse and action as a way to give the psyche a chance to grow. Eigen is an expert on creative waiting and playing for time. He uses time as a background object for support. He treats the audience to creative ways to begin to allow the psyche to grow. Dream work becomes a feature of Day 1, and Eigen speaks about how "evacuated pain finds its way into dreaming" (p. 7, Day 1). He brings together much more in his spontaneous illuminating discussion as he advocates for growth borne out of helplessness. Growth takes the form of being able to see the psyche from multiple vertices, a term borrowed from Bion. Creating a gap enables this to occur. As in the two previous Seoul seminars, the Question and Answer sessions allow Eigen to demonstrate how he walks around his own psyche, and in real time, the audience also learns how he teaches his patients to practice this as well.

Day 2 treats the audience to the mystical nature of the Kabbalah, the timeless nature of the stories and lessons, and how they link with psychoanalysis and the everyday struggles of life. Eigen devotes time to Bion, Winnicott, and Jung as he connects human nature across the centuries, then and now. Eigen draws from the mystical roots planted long ago in a story he tells about Rabbi Akiva which serves as one of the backdrops for Eigen's plea for us to pour everything we can into whatever capacity we have. The Kabbalah emphasizes a spark. Despite all our shortcomings and incapacities, everyone can make use of themselves in some way. Whatever use that may be, Eigen encourages us to use that capacity and pour our heart and souls into it. He links this to Distinction-Union, reminding us that absence or presence is not as important as what is possible in the moment. There is no absence without presence and vice-versa. He believes in moments and moments grow. "Each little bit is a doorway to immensity" (p. 9, Day 2). Eigen applies his distinction-union idea to Rabbi Nachman, describing Nachman's extreme states of feeling, "ecstatic closeness and agonized loss: heaven and the pit, the abyss" (p. 32, Day 2). These aspects are co-nourishing. Eigen throughout the day weaves Bion, Freud, Henry Elkin (Eigen's main analyst), Matte-Blanco's symmetrical/asymmetrical, "the interplay of multiple realities" (p. 26, Day 2), as portals to come to terms with constant struggle, embracing the value of the creative imbalance of our psyches, gently reminding us that balance or centering ourselves is an idealized state of being. He refuses to side with modern day words, such as "bipolar"; instead, he values the pain of the human condition and the importance of growing into the pain of multitudes. As with Day 1, the Question and Answer sessions illuminate and bring forth new koans and sparks of beauty.

Much of what Eigen teaches is how to survive the experience of being lost while alive, a paradox. He begins Day 3 observing that those that were able to show up to Day 3 were "survivors." Part of Day 3 encompasses Eigen's commentary on "Something Wrong," a play he wrote and included in *Flames from the Unconscious*. The play has been performed in the United States and in Sweden. Tomas Transtromer, a Swedish Poet wrote, "Deep in the forest there's an unexpected clearing which can be reached only by someone who has lost his way" (2006, p. 144). Themes of the play link catastrophic change with grace, brokenness with grace, a sense of something wrong in the human spirit and psyche with grace. Grace is the patient in the play. Reading Eigen interpreting his own writing is fascinating, while at the same time, discovering how being lost helps us reach the clearing, if we can survive the journey. Work with those who are lost is where Eigen lives as he, too, generously shares his own lost, "something wrong" self with the audience.

As one reads Eigen's PASSAGES during this third, three-day seminar in Seoul, Korea, one feels sparks of the Universe oscillating between then and now, inside and outside of our being, through centuries of mystics. The timelessness of themes Eigen mines knit together a thread of shared human existence and feelings that aid in us becoming better functioning containers of our feelings, while recognizing and embracing our helplessness along the way. One can't help but feel the beauty in terror, the growing nature of faith borne from tolerating pain, and the inhaling of the breath that makes it possible to feel the Universe pulsating within us. Eigen teaches us to produce and breathe our own psychic oxygen, and another moment is born.

Chapter 1

Day 1

Morning: bumping into oneself

Thanks for coming. For some of you, this is the third time that we are meeting together, so I can't possibly say anything new (Eigen, 2010, 2011a).

This morning I am going to read from, paraphrase, and talk about Chapter 1 in *Feeling Matters* (2007, pp. 11–21) called "Yosemite God." For ease of exposition I will not use quotation marks for all quotes, as often quotes, paraphrases, and amplifications are mixed. Some words will be the same as the text, others not. Sometimes the text may be like a diving board or prompt, a stimulus. And sometimes I let it speak for itself. Hopefully, something further will happen, something that may touch, be of use.

Yosemite is a national park in California, a natural park made up of immense, ancient boulders, gigantic rocks from ancient times, bare and striking, awesome. When President Theodore Roosevelt saw Yosemite Park he was prevailed upon by Edmond Muir, a dedicated naturalist, conservationist, to start setting up national protection for natural places of beauty, natural wonders. I went there on the way to visit one of my sons who was starting college in a desert near Death Valley. A world of wonder.

The ancient rocks seemed to have a life of their own. I've come to feel over time that such experiences of beauty and wonder link with other feelings that follow from them, like a wish to protect them, gratitude, care, and a need to do justice to such beauty in life. I suspect such experiences of beauty and awe are part of a natural groundwork for a sense of ethics, wanting to do right by this world that so touches us, an urge to find ways to do justice to a world and life which arouses such soul-feelings, justice to the sense of amazement that there should be such things. An urge to do existence justice.

I began thinking of other things in our experience that have some kind of relationship to ethics. One is sleep. In English there is an expression, "profound sleep," to sleep profoundly. There are times one accesses deep peace in sleep. Not the same as the hustle and bustle of much waking consciousness or even the busyness of dreams. Some think the profound peace touched in sleep may be another kind of consciousness or perhaps what we call consciousness has a rest and another domain opens. I've heard people extol moments of such deep rest and peace, grateful not just for relief and renewal but something more. I think it links with ethics because of the profound value such peace brings. A sense of peace that can spread, to some extent, through our lives.

Peace is not the only state that accesses us in sleep. And, of course, there are people whose sleep is agitated and this peace may not come to them or come but rarely. But there are many emotions that come to us in sleep, some we have names for and some we don't, subtle states beyond representational grasp which we somehow sense. We come to a point in sleep that touches us with nameless presence and possibility.

An ethics based on wonder or awe or joy or beauty or mystery. A profundity of experience that exceeds our grasp but affects us, that we almost reach, perhaps almost say or sing or dance as it elusively reaches us. Or perhaps we learn to simply bask in it and taste with all our pores in quieting, stirring stillness.

I'd like to add another moment, the experience of another's face. How many here have read Levinas? Emmanuel Levinas (1969; Eigen, 1979, 1993, 2005) has an ethics of the face. He spoke of the nakedness and vulnerability of the face. He didn't emphasize the defensive, angry, attacking aspect. He emphasized a naked, vulnerable aspect that elicits a need to do it justice. Of course, we are many things: mean, cruel, caring, many moods, and attitudes. Levinas focuses on the face that calls to us, that calls us to respond. A response that might always be beyond what we can do, an infinite call, a call that cannot be exhausted. For Levinas the other's face opens a sense of infinity. It is, I feel, a paradox of existence, that an infinite call beyond anything we can possibly do, calls into being potentialities and possibilities we might otherwise not have discovered and lived. A call for infinite care and justice, an infinite need to do justice to life, may stimulate growth of capacities that otherwise might have remained unknown. Another paradox associated with this is: the fact that there is more beyond what we can think, feel, and do can generate the wisdom that, at any time, we do not have all answers and abilities – a ground for humility in relation to one another.

The fact that we cannot do everything (there is no everything to do) does not mean that we cannot do anything. But it is a deep and important learning to be respectful of the fact that our something, however valuable, is not everything. Although for the moment, it may mean everything to a person.

We are surrounded by an ethical call, ethics that calls to us from nature, ethics that calls to us from depths of our own being, and ethics that calls to us from the infinity of the other's face. Now we know in human life that there is an awful amount of destruction and, at times, beauty and destruction go together. This afternoon I will talk about destruction and negative infinities.

But this morning, I am going to read and talk about ethics grounded in joy or beauty or awe or care, a positive sense of infinity.

* * *

Yosemite silenced me. Words dissolved. A wordless world for millions of years. What can speaking do? Tears, awe, like so many other people before me. Mammoth rocks, mammoth stars. God's beauty. The soul of the rock says, "Come closer" (2007, p. 11).

Immense rocks reverberating in your body, in your skin, deep inside. "Come closer."

A sign says, "Here is where Theodore Roosevelt camped with John Muir, spoke good forest talk, and left Roosevelt inspired to conserve remnants of nature's forests and wilderness."

So this is what words can do. Words can inspire great thoughts, feelings, actions. In people so different as Theodore Roosevelt and myself, words can and do make a difference. What I put into my writings, my books: words that echo the silence, the wind and water – the spirit that hovers.

In the beginning of the Bible, it says that God hovered over the waters. A colleague in New York, Jack Wiener, told me that "hovered" can also be translated, "trembled." God trembled. Trembling might be better, although I like them both – hovering, trembling. Spirit that trembles, uplifts, dashes down, trembles over the waters of your being, creating you anew each moment.

Not God as signifier for inbuilt, unknown intelligence. Not the rationalistic God. God that gives birth to religions. Religions that reveal and obscure. Religions that often mess up but provide hints, God-prints. Sometimes I think of religions as God fossils. Then suddenly, a fossil may come to life, lift and thrill or frighten, open reality. Or sometimes religion becomes an implant which takes root and flowers and/or strangles. As I look at the great rocks of Yosemite I wonder, are religions necessary? Isn't Yosemite enough? Doesn't Yosemite ignite God all by itself? Surely God, too, must be awed, dumbfounded, moved, swept away, by forms creation takes.

Maybe we should take religion more as a gush, an outcry, a moan, a whisper, an unfolding prayer. Like the last psalms, singing, banging drums, blowing horns. Songs that echo what life feels like when aliveness quivers and surges.

Yet religion also implants. I think of lighting Shabbos (Sabbath) candles; a holy day of rest; eating challah, a bread baked throughout my childhood; learning that rest is very special, more holy, even than repentance – on Shabbos we can rest even from repenting.

I remember the transgressive pleasure in Hebrew school a teacher took, shocking us by saying that Shabbos is even holier than Yom Kippur, the holiest day of the year, Day of Atonement. Yom Kippur a fast day, Shabbos a day of family meals. He woke us up. I thought – if you can think that, you can think anything. A weekly reminder of renewal that acts as a vehicle to access an ever-present possibility of renewal from within/without, any moment, now.

Childhood memories and implants. When they work, these plants grow and grow, and you grow with them, and the holy grows too. Too often, what might have enriched, stifles, even cripples, and one tries to start from scratch, rarely free for long from an undertow. In my life, I have to confess, the undertow has come to my rescue many times.

Awe, holiness, sense of the sacred. An immediate feeling, not a thought, not intellectual. It just rises up. When you see the rock, when you see the face, you feel a sense of the sacred. I've had this feeling from an early age, nearly as far back as I can remember. I've heard others speak about a similar thread in their lives, so it may not simply be my style. When I share these moments with others, there is often a sense of recognition.

I had this feeling the first moment I did therapy in an office alone with another person. A sacred sense. The other's face, tone, gestures, need for help. Many years ago I wrote a book (1998) in which I said psychoanalysis is a form of a prayer.

Many of our patients show us that religious implants can be destructive. A person may try to pull a bad implant out, try to break free, only to take in another bad implant. Sometimes the bad implant is psychoanalysis and one runs, trying to find something better. Sometimes we call these bad implants parents. Good and bad aspects of God, of parents, of psychoanalysis, of living. All mixed up. Blends of toxic and life-giving nourishment, often indistinguishable. Few things are more binding, more gripping than toxic nourishment (Eigen, 1999) and damaged bonds (Eigen, 2001). They have a strong hold. We use psychoanalysis, in part, to pump out our psychic stomachs and restore ability to digest experience.

Psychoanalysis runs the risk of being damaged by the damage it works with. How to build tolerance for psychic toxins so that one can work with them, approach what we fear, come closer to experiencing, challenging, working with our makeup? Psychoanalysis is less a medicine than act of creation, a process involved with incessant reshaping, re-texturing, and fine-tuning of affective attitudes.

Attitudes have feelings and feelings have attitudes. I see Jae Hoon Lee (the head of the Object Relations Institute in Seoul) has translated *Toxic Nourishment* into Korean. Emotional toxic nourishment. Something psychoanalysts, psychotherapists tend to address more than most. I think of the institute's graduation ceremony I attended today and wonder, what do psychoanalysts add, what do psychoanalysts give, what can new graduates offer? And here is something – something that has to do with emotional pain – learning, discovering, practicing useful attitudes towards psychic pain.

We try to get rid of emotional pain yet often evacuated pain finds its way into dreaming. That's one reason why many dreams are bad. We have many aborted, nightmarish dreams. Scary dreams express pain we can't handle. Emotional irritants never totally dissolve. We may try to act as if emotional irritants don't matter or may blow up in face of them. Either way we are trying to get rid of them without giving them their due. It does not seem practical to pay much attention to them. You have to make a living and such feelings get in the way. Having feelings we can't handle puts us in a bind. What's the sense of spending much time with them. We don't know what to do with them anyway. On the other hand, not paying attention has effects which may ambush us.

Psychoanalysis provides a space to pay attention to emotional irritants, to learn to work better with emotional reality. Time in therapy is set aside to experience and learn about feelings. For those minutes or hours, we can learn to think a different way than when we do when making a living or seeking influence. Little by little, dosing it out, we sit there and build tolerance for facing feelings or learn to simply experience them and gradually stay with them. Little by little, we get to know what is bothering us, or at least that something is bothering us. We learn to make room, befriend ourselves in ways we hadn't thought possible. A befriending which also involves experiencing what we are up against with, what seems intractable, damaged, and destructive.

To pay attention to what is bothering us and not assume we know it all ahead of time. Learning involves surprises. Psychotherapy is not the only or exclusive approach. Social reform, social work, and many other help modalities can play important roles on societal, individual, and familial levels. No one modality has the answer for everything. But psychotherapy with individuals brings something very important to the pool. It adds to a growing awareness of our makeup in very personal ways, how we are bothered by attitudes, capacities, and tendencies that constitute us, and explores ways of working with them.

I said before that emotional irritants never totally dissolve. They press into our dreams as well as other processes beyond our usual ways of thinking. Often we can't say what they are, but can sense their impact. Intimations of core agonies, often eluding ability to name. Odd to think of psychotherapy as marginal to our society, dealing with experiences people try to relegate to the margins of awareness – a marginal profession dealing with marginal emotions. Which very often turns out to be work with the very core of our beings. As I've often said, unless this work is assimilated in the public domain, unless what is bothersome in us is given its due, well-intended reforms and aid which help may also hit rocks of human nature that go unnoticed or are played down, but can't be wished away.

Many dreams are partially successful. Bion said all dreams are aborted dreams, aborted processes, aborted emotions or emotional sequences. If dreaming is part of our emotional digestive system, we get an awful lot of emotional indigestion. Feelings we try to work with get aborted. In such cases, dreams take emotions part of the way, then cut off. We are left with a sense of incompletion. Starting and stopping. A broken off rhythm that applies to many dimensions, including aborted or interrupted lives or aspects of living. Kafka called his life an incomplete moment. From this perspective, perhaps, all moments are incomplete.

I suggested that far from being at the margins of society, psychotherapy is at a center. There are many centers. Our emotional core or cores exercise pressures hard to pin down. Dreams are part of a dramatic core, dramatic emotional core, sometimes offering possibilities for growth without necessarily solving anything. We cannot "solve" our nature but we can partner with it, work with it, learn with it.

To have a successful dream is not just to feel better or to succeed in wish fulfillment, but to nibble, to nibble on what is bothering us a little more. Dreams are like fish nibbling little trauma pieces, sooner or later bringing you to nameless irritants built into life. Nameless irritants that are parts of the way life is made. Life as an irritant – a pleasure and irritant.

In the Garden of Eden, an image of paradise, there were already limitations, irritation, tantalization. Enjoy but don't touch the fruit. No was already in paradise. Look how beautiful, but don't touch, don't eat the fruit of knowledge. And after touching, eating the fruit of knowledge – don't go near the tree of life! Some paradise! Maybe our ideas about what paradise should be need some revision.

How to put this? We wouldn't be here without limitation, without form. We are a forming process. Nothing exists as a form without limit. And we experience the limit as pressing us. The limits that enable us to be also irritate us. So nibbling on what is bothering us sooner or later brings us past our bad society, past our bad parents – brings us to a nameless irritant that helps structure our bad parents and society. Everything we say is bad about society or our parents may be real, but prevents us from going farther and seeing that what bothers us is built into life itself. An agony that remains invisible no matter how one names it.

Exploding dream bubbles challenge us to be an artist of the invisible, with materials like but not limited to trauma clots that aborted dreams nibble on. Barely felt, barely sensed trauma bits that affect us but often elude ability to name.

* * *

I'd like to return to Yosemite God (bottom of page 12). The God I know wants us to create, to taste the power that makes us giddy. What would "giddy" be? Excited, thrilled, drunk? Giddy with God, harmless with others. Jesus comments to his disciples that they be harmless as doves, smart as snakes. To be harmless with others – something that will never happen. A wish. The best we can do, I suspect, is to do what's a little less harmful. I am thinking of a form of addiction therapy which does not work by total abstinence, but slow steps at a time, first a little less addicted, a little less more (Tatarsky, 2007). A little less self-harm at a time. Does God want us to practice something that will never happen – to be harmless? A harm-free existence? I doubt there is a single soul in this world that is harmless. Does God want us to achieve the impossible – a world without murder?

I was once studying with two old Kabbalists in Brooklyn years ago. Their picture of heaven was that here on earth, after the Messiah came, if someone picked up his hand to strike another, an angel would appear and stop the hand in mid-air. It would not be possible for one man to strike another – ever. Maybe some think we can do better than that, but so far we haven't done that well.

We create psychoanalysis to recreate ourselves. If not to recreate ourselves, at least to try to help ourselves, or at least to work with ourselves. I said we, but of course, I mean Freud. Once a tool leaves its maker's hand, anyone can use it. How to use it is still a question.

I picture God telling the heavenly hosts, "Let's send them Freud with the hope they'll do a better job with their impulses." Floods and plagues didn't work. Religions didn't work. Still the same old bunch of killers – soul killers, financial killers, just plain killers.

The other day a therapist was telling me about a case in Texas, someone who came for therapy from a fundamentalist group. Her father beat her and her siblings and kept on beating them. When he would get tired, he would pray to have the strength to keep on beating. So – religion is no protection from ourselves, our killing or hurtful nature. The promise of heaven for good behavior, hell for bad – sometimes this gets all mixed up.

Here comes psychoanalysis for another try, working with impulses in freer, indirect ways. With free associations, free-floating attention, saying what you want, listening in new ways. Listening to yourself in new ways. Perhaps psychoanalysis wants to teach us how to be bad in better ways, less destructive ways. Since psychoanalysis came into the world there have been two world wars and global hostilities that seem endless. So far its presence has not done the trick on a global level but some people have been helped (some harmed).

It may be that what psychoanalysis teaches has not been grasped in full enough, real enough ways. What is real is power. And power, as practiced in a world of economic and territorial competition, involves killing. Psychoanalysis, by comparison, for all its emphasis on destructiveness, seems utopian. Even though its words are witness to mixed realities from beginning to end.

As we work with this new toy, psychoanalysis, we find much more than simple impulse control is at stake. An ideology of control, mental or international, is insufficient. Impulses break through control. In the society I know, impulse control is a big thing in bringing up children, but that doesn't stop adults from doing awful things. The impulsivity of society is enormous. An ideology of control seems pathetic in a psychopathic world. A control model was tried for hundreds, perhaps thousands of years, but did not do the trick. One can say things would have been even worse without it. It put some bridle on the masses. The fact it did not solve the problem of murder does not make it useless. Struggling with oneself, trying to hold back impulses can play a role in healing – e.g., working with a rager (Eigen, 2002). To a certain extent, brute struggle to hold back and control oneself can help up to a point, and is necessary at a certain stage. But free associating in sessions and building a psychic network of meaning and feeling play a crucial role in control being possible. The psychic work with an addictive rager, for example, can build a net of meaning and feeling that puts a gap between the raging impulse and action. A gap that can lead to richer alternatives.

For one thing, paradoxically, a new experience of a gap between impulse and action can lead to a sense of fullness. A richer, fuller sense of life, rich with possibility, in marked contrast with the rigid straitjacket and helplessness of compulsive raging. A possibility of experiencing more feeling instead of being buffeted, pummeled, thrown about by it.

After some psychic work, sometimes I tell ragers to freeze, be paralyzed, wait, just wait, and wait. Don't even think. Don't try to figure it out. Intellect may help but is not enough. Insights like my mother beat me and now I beat my child may play a role but usually do not do the trick. Something more is needed. Letting associative networks build plays a role in sustaining a gap that can be widened by doing nothing. Squeeze yourself, go blank, go dead. Extend a moment of waiting, so psyche has a chance to grow. In time, with support, the psyche supports more feeling. Support begets support. Richness begins to spread.

In one case, a man compulsively screamed at his wife. "I'm right, I'm right," he felt and believed. "I screamed because she handed me a cold bottle to feed the baby. How could she! Didn't she know the bottle was cold?!" He felt his screaming was justified. In *Rage* (2002) I wrote, nothing has done more harm in human history than the sense of being right. He completes feeding the baby and as soon as he lay the baby down to sleep screamed at her some more, then hit his hand against the wall, damaging both wall and hand. A gesture of control of sorts, also menacing, with the implicit threat of what he could do to her.

Thinking about it is not enough, control in this case useless. What is needed, too, is opening a whole new field of experience. A field of experience that is not so one-tracked, a sense of something more important and richer than being right. Being "right" keeps him tight and mad. How can one develop more tracks, a larger network of psychic possibilities, a tolerance for more than a contracted sense of rightness, a contraction that magnifies? A magnified sense of right fuels rage.

In therapy interaction there can be questions, a sense of back and forth that, to some extent, keeps the experiential field at least a little more open. You can point out when he shuts down, shuts out. Feel the signals preceding the blowup, like sensing an epileptic fit. Slowing down to feel the signals. Little by little a beginning gap between impulse and act grows. Not the least of it being giving someone a chance to talk with another person who weathers storms, neither cowed nor vengeful. Another person who keeps dialogue potentially open, at least somewhat open, more than someone is used to. One cannot quite get satisfaction from tyrannizing when there is no one to tyrannize. Over time, one begins to sense ways he cruelly tyrannizes himself, at the mercy of his own pain and tumult.

One learns to walk around oneself, akin to walking around a sculpture and seeing it from different points of view. A rager restricts himself to one point of view but often there are latent possibilities for multiple perspectives that can be encouraged and brought out. This partly hinges on sustaining interaction so that seeing things from various viewpoints has a chance to grow. A kind of inner battle between tyranny and democracy, in which the latter for some time has little say. One may wish for a more democratic psyche but be unable to let it happen. Perhaps a function of therapy, in that case, is to sustain the hope in the latter's possibility, if not now, someday. Often a year's work can form a decent beginning. Once some improvement is tasted, more is possible.

Do you remember the last time I was here (Eigen, 2011), I talked about a psychotic patient of Bion's who had a fit because the waitress (I almost said, the witness) gave him half a cup of coffee? How could she do this! She spoiled the whole evening! He could not recover. Imagine – half a cup! For him that was worse than nothing at all. In such a moment, impulse drowned out psyche. Like a little boy in a temper tantrum (Eigen, 2004). The little boy may promise to be good and be good for a time, but the impulse eventually overwhelms and he throws a fit. The term "he throws a fit" is somewhat misleading. Actually, it is more like a fit throws him. Control alone is not the answer. It simply does not work well enough. For something like generative self-restraint to develop, a deeper field of psychic possibilities must form the background of one's being. The model of control that has dominated society so long promotes warp rather than warmth. Neither control nor impulse indulgence nor their fusions is the answer. We need to get outside the box of that model and let the psyche grow. We can do better than becoming impulsive, angry adults, good one moment, mad the next.

What can psychoanalysis contribute that's different? Bion said that no one has ever yet assessed what the psychoanalytic method is. Whatever tries one has made are insufficient because we keep learning more about what we can do with this toy or tool. Processes called psychoanalysis are not static. Formulations one points to at one time aren't good enough for the kinds of things that swim into view at another point. Bion describes psychoanalysis as a baby, still unknown, sometimes murderous and parasitic and also creative, fresh, new. We may not know what kinds of processes are at work in the background, facilitating birth and growth or destruction. We sense what we can, midwife what we can, and learn what we can as we go along. Formulas are not enough. They can't keep up with living reality.

In the first chapter of *Contact with the Depths* (2011a), I discuss a case in which I did not know what was happening. I feared I might be contributing to something destructive yet waited it out, contributing a kind of supportive affective background for dramas the patient experienced. It took about eight months of radical unknowing before the process began to crystallize into something clearly valuable. Now, years later, I would call that a kind of waiting in faith. A complex faith which supports the patient as largely unconscious processes work at psychic growth, akin to a dream cocoon, until an experience is ready to be born. A lot of unseen processes lead up to visible birth.

We are growing with psychoanalysis and psychoanalysis is growing with us. Fields of intertwining, pulsing, rigid, shifting affective attitudes swim in and out of view. Glimpses of emotional worlds, nuances of feeling, and then in a blink, nothing, a void, fissures of consciousness with intimations of unconscious life. We make inferences about unconscious processes, using gaps in consciousness as tea leaves. We try to make coherent narratives out of networks of lines and holes, prematurely ordering elusive hints, ironing out signs of incoherence. Many dreams are fragments of dreams we prematurely complete with ideas about them. For Bion both the dream and ideas can be viewed as hypotheses bringing things together in various ways. A dream itself may be an interpretation of experience that our available equipment cannot reach. If we learned anything about the world, it is that unknown realities can impact us in ways we do not know. Psychoanalysis credits this possibility and takes it seriously as part of its method. Bion calls the psychoanalytic attitude faith and describes it as being without memory, expectation and desire, openness to impacts and transformations in O, his notation for unknowable, ultimate emotional reality.

Attention turns to nuances of emotional transmissions, especially unconscious emotional transmissions which cannot be known but may be lived. How we live in relation to larger, unknown fields that make us up and support or pummel us is, at least somewhat, open to scrutiny, construction, interpretation. We assume we are living in psychic realities where feelings swim back and forth in many or all directions, psychic seas beyond observation. Formulations come to us as we spend time with someone. Suppose we are with someone we sense is disturbed by immense self-hate and threatened by destructive feelings. We may say something that takes the edge off self-punishment for the moment and in so doing enable a larger view of life and self to appear. It is paradoxical that there are moments when awareness of one's self-hate in a larger context enables one to feel freer. For many, whatever one says or doesn't say, the work involves, in the long run, emotional transmission of something good in face of the destructive laceration of oneself an individual has fallen into. Better feeling gets through over time that offsets, more than before, bad feelings that plague a life, resulting in a greater degree of affective flow and possibilities.

You might talk about the weather, the temperature outdoors or in the room. The psyche knows you are talking about feeling. You might talk about the Oedipus complex or envy, or whatever myths or events you are comfortable with. Often what is real for you communicates the possibility of something being real for the patient. What is real for you might not be real for the patient but the fact that something feels real *does* get communicated. Such talk provides a larger context for a sense of real, as the latter here tends to occur in less toxic ways. A sense of creative real has a chance to grow to offset destructive real.

In another case or time, accepting a sense of unreal may need room. Insistence on real when unreal needs space can be stifling.

We are very permeable, even if we rigidly try to shut out feeling. Even a stone is stained by weather and some of these colors we call beautiful. Sometimes we have to push away in order to let in. There is a battle within between feeling worse and better. Often good feeling is not trusted if it has been used to fob off discomfort. There is a range-finder inside that senses whether to go forward or backward, raise or lower the emotional volume, touch or keep distance, move towards or away and with what quality, what tone.

A person may be struggling to find a working balance between letting in and keeping out, between permeability and evacuation. We are very sensitive and can't bear very much. We tone down our sensitivity in order to survive. In some instances, we kill ourselves off in order to survive. A graveyard of the self exists that haunts personality in the background, sometimes foreground. Moments of annihilation while growing up congeal. Most of us survive our own annihilation and go on living in better and/or worse ways. It makes some difference if we can make room for what we had to "give up" in order to live. Some are unable to mourn for themselves, which can make for a certain brittleness or abrasive toughness. The conjunction celebrate-mourn working together makes a difference in tone of personality. Maybe this is something Walt Whitman touched on in his own way, celebrating himself (his experience) yet writing much on death (perhaps the greatest experience of all). Here we touch not just the death ahead but the deaths that have already happened. The tone of our personality partly depends on quality of approach in both directions.

Bion, one way or another, often asks how much experience we can take. We oscillate between permeability and trying to evacuate sensitivity. To what extent does unconscious processing try to get rid of itself? Is the pain and damage that runs through personality bearable? Bion raises the possibility of dream work getting damaged, so that unconscious processing cannot process. One is frozen, jammed, deformed. Psyche suffers malignancies, psychic cancers. We rely on unconscious processing to support our conscious life. Yet, to some degree, our psyche is subject to murder (Eigen, 1996).

I suspect we have come some way from common sense and legalistic thinking. Winnicott as well as Bion emphasized the importance of dream work. Both connect dream work to processing emotional experience. Winnicott, also, to creating it. Bion, also, sees a creative dimension to dreaming, although he tends to emphasize creativity up against destructive forces. Winnicott writes a lot about relations between destruction-creation (Eigen, 2012, 2013). Both have been influenced by Freud's and Melanie Klein's writings on the destructive urge and seek ways to meet it (Eigen, 2010 Eigen in Seoul 1) Freud wrote of dreams as a royal road to the unconscious. In their own special ways, Winnicott and Bion take the pulse of the psyche partly through dreams.

Awareness of the importance of dream work grew. Winnicott felt dreaming contributes to the use of experience, making life feel real. Bion connects dream work to processing emotional experience. We have to dream life into reality. Damaged dream work leaves us in a state of chronic emotional indigestion or shut down. For Bion something like dream work goes on day and night, linking levels and forms of existence, taking life in, working it over, giving back in profound interweaving.

But there is, too, experience beyond dreaming. Dreaming is already on the road to narrative structures and rationalization we can work with while awake. Dreams often, perhaps usually, have narrative structure of some kind. They tend to go from here to there in some way. Someone tries to get through the door and attack me. That's a narrative like a crime story, a scary movie. Narrative is one of the ways we give coherence to life. We have our stories and some of our stories serve better than others. Some of our stories constrict our lives, make our lives more rigid.

I don't know what you know about American politics. The Tea Party has narratives, and progressives have narratives. Their narratives appear to have little in common, yet each group believes in its narratives. Perhaps it is like each group believing in a different dream. Dreams that give coherence and structure to social reality. That we are meaning making beings has dangers. We go to war over our meanings. We fight each other over meanings, your picture or story over mine. We fight over ways we give coherence to reality. In some sense, we fight over our dreams.

Dreams come to us through semi-narrative processes. We know that narratives and dreams select and emphasize certain bits of the field of experience and neglect others. Selection and shaping processes spontaneously occur then often harden into specific viewpoints. Enduring organizations of meaning tend to prejudice us with regard to how we experience experience. There are vast potentials in the field of experience that our narratives miss. Narratives are a little like ladles drawing cups of possibilities from wells of meaning. Words fish in the emotional unconscious. Words are multi-directional, at once pinpointing what is seen and heard, while steeped in mystery. Words work with consciousness while rooted in unconscious wonder. Often they carry a sense of triumph or mastery: "We've got you, a little bit of you." Often, they simmer with frustration for all that cannot be gotten.

We try to mold the vast unconscious with our narratives, the fish we've managed to net. We may try to live our lives by our stories, our beliefs. They may serve well or ill, depending on their usefulness with regard to a particular stage, level, or dimension of living. A narrative that works for a child of five may not work for the man of fifty. A story that works for one child of five may not work for another. Different sensibilities and stories that mold and express them may be part of the background in shaping political and aesthetic groups. We tend to hold on to the way we structure experience, although this way of putting it is a little misleading. The way experience gets structured tends to exceed our will and efforts. We tend to hold on to the way our experience is structured or it holds us, very often to our disadvantage. The way we are organized lets us live but sometimes does not let us live very well.

So, dream as narrative structure that gives coherence to realities that remain vastly unknown. Even scientists are finding that they do not know what matter is and postulate that most matter is unknown, dark matter. Even if most of the universe and its processes are unknown, we know enough to make a building like one we are in, and to help many patients who come to see us in this building. We know enough to try to talk together as we are today. We know enough to make atom bombs and to build amazing technology.

Look at everyone – everyone is texting. I can easily envision a time or need to text with a patient in the same room. Texting when together may be the only way to get through to some people. Some people will be so uncomfortable talking intimately they will need to text with you. There are young people unable to communicate verbally with their strong emotions but can text about them somewhat more and write all night about them on the internet. They may be stymied with you face to face, but bring out a smart phone and the world opens up. They light up phone to phone.

Back to dreaming and beyond dreaming. There is a place in sleep deeper than dreams, deeper than our usual organizations and narratives. We sleep not only to dream, but to contact places that dreaming can't reach. Dreams are important. But also important are places that dreaming can't access, that dreaming fails to package. A dimension in sleep outside our usual patterns. (Eigen, 2007, Chapter 1).

There are experiences outside of dreaming's reach and some of these experiences reach towards dreaming. Some experiences outside of dreaming's reach, reach towards dreaming to be dreamt into narratives that feed us, for use we can make of them.

I think of the Hindu saying that everyday life is the past, dreaming is the present, and dreamless void, the future. We might call part of dreamless void a wordless, imageless unconscious through which our lives are impalpably and ineffably fed by experience that accesses us in dreamless sleep. Dreamless sleep feeds our lives. Certain kinds of states access us through dreamless sleep that waking can obscure. As though God or nature or evolution has safeguarded, has kept something safe from our use of it.

We help create but also plunder experience. We tend to grab and exploit what is given us for use. In a way, unconscious life, unconscious void, guards experiencing from consciousness. Such intricate dramas go on between "systems," the hide and seek of the psyche. The system that Freud called "Ich" or "ego" can be a predator. The "vast unconscious" needs protection from ego's prying and, at times, corrupting ways (as does the external world). Dreamless sleep as a special form of renewal, a special form of contact that we cannot ruin with our controlling narratives or lust for power or our fears. Something in us kept safe from ourselves. Something safe inside, that gains access to us when ordinary focus, attention, narratives, even the narratives of our dreams, are out of play. A special form of contact that accesses us when we're not looking.

Freud wrote of the importance of sleeping-dreaming: we can dream things in our sleep which would be dangerous (to do) while awake. Sleep protects us from acting when under emotive sway of the dreaming unconscious. Here we touch another area, reaching dimensions that access us without images, narratives, or concepts, a very precious area of experiencing. A sutra I love speaks of Buddha lands that are wordless, unconceptualized, unimaginable, unrepresentable – yet through it transformative work goes on. You can sometimes sense it, have intimations. And you can feel changed by it, if you don't impede it with your narratives.

QUESTION 1: We talked about the dream having a narrative structure and I agree with this idea. However in sessions, I have the experience where the patient does not really understand his or her own narratives in the dream. Can you help me cope with this situation?

RESPONSE 1: No two moments are alike. Whatever comes to you at the moment – you'll try to see what your intuition brings at a particular time. I wouldn't put a burden on a person – here the burden of understanding his/her dreams. It's like an unspoken commandment: "Thou shalt understand your dream." A kind of prosecutorial position. Both you and the patient will feel persecuted by the dream, by a demand for understanding. It's enough to wonder about the dream, the dream brings a sense of wonder, puzzlement. That can be lost too quickly by demanding comprehension, premature closure.

One possibility is to see if some parts of a dream strike you. Maybe you like or are curious about a certain image, or color, or word, fragment. Something that might arouse you to say, "Wow, I'm curious about this. How do you like this image or word or color or thought?" Or, "Wow, this is scary – a fearful happening." Underlining action or affect, making subtitles. "Wow, that is beautiful."

> I'd love to hear a little more from the dream or some part of it. What would it say? I used to work with a man who invited us to play different parts of the dream, make believe we were people or objects in the dream.
>
> (Perls, 1969)

You can pick a part of the dream, even an inanimate object, or a scene, or a mood and say, "Tell me everything you can about X, everything you remember your whole lifelong." If nothing, you can suggest making something up. If that doesn't work, you can speak of your own feelings about this are that dream element, something that touches you or awakens wonder. There is much that can happen without trying for understanding. Many ways to begin letting the dream or parts of it in. The dream feeling is sometimes more important than meanings we make up for it. You are limited only by your own imagination.

> Feeling bad or persecuted by not understanding a dream can be an important feeling in other areas of a person's life. One might use the dream to open up a taste of feeling and possibility - one can appreciate a dream without necessarily having to understand it. Open a little bit and let it go. Find something that will not be shaming or, if shaming, see where shaming takes one. "Tell me everything you can remember about being shamed." "When was the first time you remember having a feeling like that?" Perhaps an individual is ashamed of incapacity – in this case capacity to understand dreams. It is easy to rub one's nose in incapacity, even without meaning to. Some speak more easily of events rather than feelings. Often the events they speak of carry the feeling. Kind of like play therapy with adults, only the "toys" are the person's life.

For some, capacity to work with dreams may develop over time. It may rub off on them through osmosis, with therapy exposure. For others, not so much. In a way, the whole session is a dream. Ancients say life is a dream. Almost anything one does involves work with dreams, dream expression. Sometimes you might ask, "Can you say a little more about that?" Maybe yes, maybe no. It's a question a person may get more used to over time and find less threatening or, later, even welcoming.

Gradually, over time, a person may begin to link dreams with life, past, present, future. Capacity is uneven with lacunae. Some have dream talent, some not. There are many kinds of talent. Maybe try to work with what a person can do rather with what they can't. Dreams often rub noses in wounds. They may be trying to communicate something that's off, especially trauma aspects of dreams. Dreams are persecutory enough. It may be a relief when a nice dream comes along.

A lot has to do with intuition, your range-finder. If you are struck by something in a dream, some part of it – you are free to share your interest as long it is not a demand. If you have responses you think worth saying, even silly ones, couch it along the lines, "Here's what I see..." Meltzer called it musing aloud. Shared reverie. Here's what I heard – but you know, I'm a therapist, and therapists get these crazy thoughts.

Don't try to do too much. Little by little, a person may begin to catch on – ah, so this is how dreams work. Or perhaps dreams will always be opaque to a person. With therapy exposure over time, something may get through, something transmitted through the dream of therapy, a shift in affective attitude hard to pin down in words.

It might also be helpful to keep in mind that, one way or another, we are working with emotional incapacities. Perhaps it takes some pressure off to realize we may be helping to build capacity over time. There are no real rules on this. Support is necessary. Now more supportive, now more challenging. Be careful not to challenge a capacity that is not there. Bear in mind, the person you are working with very likely is unaware of the ins and outs of emotional incapacity. Nevertheless, one may bump up against the latter without knowing what it is.

Somewhere Bion wrote a passage about a baby bumping its foot against the crib bars and feeling pain without knowing what it is or where it comes from, lacking orientation for the pain and surroundings. He will come to know that if he kicks the crib in a certain way, pain comes. It takes time to organize a frame of reference to situate unexpected pain and place it in a viable context: pain in my foot because it bumped the crib too hard. Something similar may happen with someone who lacks a viable frame for emotional pain. He bumps his soul or being or sensitivity against a psychic event and does not have capacity to organize it well. Why am I in pain? One might not even know he was in pain or what to do with it. People try all sorts of things when bumped by emotional pain – often intense, chronic pain in the background that now and then becomes inescapable. Blaming is one common tactic. Often, beliefs about emotional pain settle into a narrow system that locks the pain in rather than actually working with it. Or perhaps a belief system can help bypass or disregard it for shorter or longer periods unless it becomes insistent. We bump against pain in the dark, emotional pain. If only – if only this or that would happen, the pain would go away.

I don't think we – the human race – have solved difficulties associated with what emotional pain is, where it is coming from, what to do with it. We keep bumping up against ourselves and each other. We manage to make sense of it, but often the sense we make does not "solve" the difficulty, if a solution exists. Bion feels that emotions for adults who come to therapy may be somewhat like an infant bumping against an unknown object. Our relation to our emotional life has a long way to go.

What does one do in the meantime? We give ourselves and each other what support and challenge we can. Support and stimulation. Sometimes a little psychic exercise helps – finding something interesting to say, an imaginative moment that arouses a new nuance of feeling or perspective. Even sitting and waiting out a storm can help, drowsily over time, but with patience, persistence, openness and flexibility, capacity may grow.

* * *

If there are no questions, in the few minutes left this morning I'm going to work a little more with a passage beginning at the bottom of page 15 (Chapter 1, *Feeling Matters*). I was linking the beauty and awe of nature with profound, dreamless sleep in which we access feeling that eludes us during waking consciousness. A thread links the thrill of beauty in waking life with ineffable depths of sleep. This thread, I feel is connected with certain great ideas in history, e.g., Plato's Idea of the Good, Kant's treating each other as ends, not just means.

The first time I met Socrates I was a sophomore in college. When I was growing up in Passaic, New Jersey, when I heard someone use the word "truth," I usually wondered, "What do they want?" When my parents used that word, they wanted me to behave in a certain way. And so it continued on the playground and in school and social life. Truth was a peg in manipulative, even exploitive discourse. No wonder, when I was old enough, I saw through politics as a matter of course – the use of truth as lies to get one's way. Truth as a con-game, an ego-device, egocentric "truth." I grew up with mistrust of the word or, at least, the way it was used. Cynical perhaps, realistic – a word largely to cajole, seduce, intimidate, dominate. I was brought to another place upon meeting Socrates. Perhaps for the first time in my life, the first time I was totally conscious of it, I felt truth real, something I believed.

Socrates lit me up. A sense of truth lit me up. Born instantly, mediated by the great midwife of innate truth awareness. A field of truth, beauty, justice, goodness. What Plato spoke about and the way he spoke about it resonated with my whole being. It was, above all, Socrates that reached me. Something in me deeply relaxed – ah, that's more like it. This is real. Words that come from and express profound experiences that have to do with good, beauty, truth, justice. Kant's reworking of the golden rule connects with this feeling. When you have this deep sense of beauty, goodness, truth, you want to do right by it, to do justice to it.

I think psychoanalysis is deeply beautiful. For me, psychoanalysis/psychotherapy has very deep beauty and I try to do right by it and share how beautiful it is. How can something be so beautiful when it is dealing with such awful things? I hope some of you resonate, find, and live it. It can nourish a life.

So, Plato's vision of the Good is one great idea in history that links up with the Yosemite rocks and profound dreamless sleep. And Kant's treating each other as ends in themselves, not only means is another. Kant speaks of the ethical universe as being more beautiful than the starry skies above. Ineffable, impalpable, awesome beauty. Buber's I and Thou (1937) personalizes a difference Kant touches, emphasizing transformative aspects of meeting.

Where does the idea of peace, caring, treating each other as precious living beings come from in a world permeated by survival needs, practicality, antagonism, lust for power? Yet both are real. And both are mixed. When the two dimensions work well together they add to plasticity. We need to be uplifted and transformed, to help and be helped. And we need "know-how." Buber's I-Thou and I-it. We have double capacities, dual-multi-dimensions. This is part of what makes us the kind of creatures that can survive almost anywhere on the planet, in all kinds of conditions.

A problem with our psychic plasticity is it can adapt so well to an environment that it loses ability to use capacities that were not needed. If and when conditions change in major ways, under-used capacities may be weak from lack of exercise and not up to the task. You find yourself in a larger or other environment you don't have resources for, like a fish out of water. Ah, but perhaps a new kind of respiratory system can develop. There are wonderful depiction by Gabriel García Márquez (1967) of historical delusions that work well in one period that doom a culture when the momentum of history shifts and new delusions are necessary.

A variant Bion raises is that the very use of capacities that develop in one situation may work against living in another. He cites the armor of the Stegosaur or inbuilt weaponry, the teeth and claws of Tyrannosaur.

The hyper-development of capacities provides protection and advantages under one set of conditions, unable to cope in another. Bion wonders if aspects of the human mind, a new toy in history, will hypertrophy at the expense of other aspects and lead to its own extinction.

We have so many capacities that support and conflict with each other. So many possibilities. How to use them? Do we get stuck in smaller, localized adaptations or find ways of partnering our capacities so that a larger frame remains open? We have plasticity for smaller and larger views simultaneously. Can we develop a larger attitude as a frame with which to partner both over-used and under-used capacities? How to expand our emotional field while able to work with the situation at hand?

Aggression, power, lust, greed – where would we be without them? Bion writes of the importance, too, of creativity greed. Beauty, justice, care, goodness – where would we be without them? Aggression is necessary for nourishment. Aggression can be nourishing. This has emotional correlates as well, mixtures, as Freud envisioned, e.g., fusions of aggression and love in sexuality, in erotic nourishment. In Kabbalah the Tree of Knowledge is also Tree of Beauty, including erotic beauty and the beauty of Eros. Eros, Cupid – with painful arrows, with joy and sorrows.

At this point of evolution, I suspect we don't know what to do with ourselves. We have lots of capacities but unsure how to relate to them. There are situations analogous to now knowing where pain is coming from. One scenario Bion depicts is the mind tearing at itself, trying to rip unlocalizable pain out. Destroying itself unable to locate the pain it wants to destroy, evacuate, tone down, get rid of. To what extent can we develop capacity that can begin to provide less destructive frames of reference for (1) unlocalized pain; (2) unnamed, nameless pain; or (3) named pain? What kinds of frames of reference (attitudes) can help us with emotion as a problem? What kinds of affective attitudes can help us with affects? How do we relate to our capacities, make room for them, use them? I think psychoanalysis has some potential for trying to explore ways of working with our emotive capacities, so that each has a voice and contribution to make. Whether or not that can happen in reality or not is another question. But cultivation of a partnership model is an attitude worth trying.

* * *

Afternoon: helpless against helplessness

If we had more time I would say more about Levinas and the ethics of the face, but this afternoon we are going to deal more with destruction, taking off from Bion's "arm falling off" dream (Bion, 1994, p. 231; Eigen, 2011, Chapter 7). Bion writes that his patient tells him a dream of being on a railway train. Looking out the window, he sees cars nearing an intersection ahead and fears a collision. He sticks his arm out the window to signal the engineer to stop the train. Or is he signaling the cars ahead to stop? The gesture is the stop signal one makes while driving a car. Unfortunately, his arm fell off in the attempt to warn, in the attempt to help, to avert disaster. To the annoyance of other passengers, the train has to stop to retrieve the arm.

We don't know if this is a real patient or a scene Bion made up. In either case, certain elements are conjoined and that is the main thing. By means of the dream Bion depicts an affect pattern. Wanting to help, or thinking one wants to help, leads to disaster while trying to ward off disaster. One disaster is substituted for another.

When I was here two years ago, we went over the half cup of coffee incident (Bion, 1994, p. 79; Eigen, 2004, Chapter 4, 2011b). The waitress brings Bion's patient half a cup and the latter feels the night is ruined. His good time turns irredeemably bad. "That finished it." An affective structure Bion communicated was something good turning bad, good feeling followed by bad feeling. Something goes wrong.

Maybe you know patients with such a pattern. Maybe you know it from yourself. It is a common experience. In the "arm falling off" dream, the wish to help is conjoined with its opposite. Helping makes things worse. There is, too something delusional about thinking one can successfully signal the engineer to stop the train by waving one's hand out the window. The means chosen by the dream is not likely to be effective in reality. An attempt to avert catastrophe leads to further difficulty. I recall a Sumerian proverb, "I escape the wild boar only to be confronted by the wild ox."

One might say he sacrificed his arm to avoid a crash. At the same time, the loss of his arm was a spontaneous happening. Nothing visibly cut it off. It fell off by itself as if signaling its own ineffectiveness. If you want to try to stop a train, if you want to signal the engineer that something is wrong, there is usually a cord to pull for that purpose. It was as if the mind confounded two situations – car signal as warning with train heading for a feared collision. We compress situations that may or may not fit. What works in one situation may not be appropriate in another. Our mind fuses elements of experience, sometimes enriching and sometimes to our detriment. If I can stop a car this way, I can stop a train this way. This kind of thinking is more prevalent than you might imagine.

A politician or head of state caught in this thought form can cause real harm by confusing signals. Loss of lives hang in the balance when mixing things up. It is often difficult to read each other's signals, all the more so when our signals are confused or mistaken about reality. If we become aware how easily we can misconstrue what may be advantageous with what is injurious, we can develop better safeguards to check ourselves. Freud spoke of reality testing, only too aware how we mix fantasy and reality.

To put one's hand out a window to stop a train looks a little like psychotic thinking. It sounds grandiose to think one will stop a train this way. It might seem strange but we do this kind of thing in lots of ways. The dream demonstrates the counterpart of power with an image of powerlessness – the arm that is supposed to help falls off. The helping hand leads to trouble. This seems something of a variant of a mythic theme, the coupling of grandiosity and injury. One, too, ought not to underplay a sense of helplessness. The dreamer may have felt panicky helplessness in face of perceived or imagined danger and impulsively did what he could at the moment. He did not, could not, think it through. An act of hysteria, fear, desperation. Grandiosity-helplessness go together.

When I was a little boy, I would put my arm out of the window when my mother was driving a car. Sometimes I stuck my head out the window, and my mother and father would say, "Don't stick your hand out. Don't stick your head out. It'll get cut off." In Bion's patient's dream it fell off by itself.

In a way, he acted like a little boy who thought he knew more about a situation than he did. As if having a little knowledge about the world made you feel you knew everything about all situations. One tends to over-generalize. What works in one situation may not work in another.

When I was a little boy, there were moments I feared my penis would fall off. Endless cycles of dying and resurrecting. It is hard to miss a reference to some kind of castration in the arm falling off dream. Perhaps a mysterious form of self-castration or warning that one cannot (fully) control the spontaneous promptings of one's being, of one's organs. It looks like the arm does not want to do what the personality chooses. The arm may have objections that went unheard. Perhaps it did not want to be part of the scenario the dreamer conjured. A rebellious arm. Instead of cooperating, it turned against, a measure of non-compliance. Perhaps it demonstrated a kind of wisdom showing the impotence of the dream ego's "solution." There are times your body may not want to do what you want to it and often it pays to listen. If you strong-will your psyche, it may push back, even to the point of injury.

The half cup of coffee incident is another variant of the basic affective structure Bion is pointing to. The patient is having an enjoyable evening until the waitress brought half a cup. He became indignant. "That absolutely finished it…I couldn't do a thing after that, Not a thing…That finished it" (1994, p. 79; Eigen, 2004, p. 62).

In another instance, someone throws a mug of beer on the patient's face while he was having an enjoyable lunch (1965, pp. 2–4; Eigen, 2004, pp. 62–63). Another in which a mother is cutting off money for the valuable analysis, ending it (1994, p. 29). Or Bion's example of ice cream (good taste of life) turning into I scream, which finally turns into silence, no feeling at all (1970, pp. 13–14).

In all these examples, you have a dramatic negative happening spoiling goodness, changing one's mood from good to bad, often with a sense that one will never recover. Bion is illustrating a "constant conjunction" – certain events go together. He means this in the way that certain events in a myth go together. For example, Garden of Eden. Everything seems nice until the bad thing happens. Or Tower of Babel, people cooperating, building together until a God-force wipes out their linking capacity. From a psychoanalytic point of view, whether God, mother, a stranger, or the force of one's own emotional trajectory, a common pattern emerges, involving building-breaking, going from good to bad or going from bad to worse. Bion touches a configuration that requires serious attention.

The more attention is paid, the more threads and nuances we see. How can we go farther or are we stuck with this good to bad structure. If the latter, becoming more aware of it might add – unless the very attempt to see ourselves makes things worse rather than better. Let us, for the moment, assume that is not always the case. Perhaps seeing more opens more possibilities, for better and/or worse. The more rooms we go into, the more doors to other rooms are seen.

Bion points out that in the dream image, the patient was not responsible for piloting the train. He wanted to be helpful, afraid he saw a danger the engineer did not. He was a passenger, not driver. When I was a child, I spent a lot of time in the backseat of a car. My mother drove (my father was afraid to drive, afraid of running into someone or something). I couldn't wait to drive. When I was a teen and qualified I never stopped driving, just as when I was younger, I never stopped riding my bike. Yet being a passenger was not always bad. It had advantages. In the back, one is not responsible for the car's movements. One can look out the window (dogs love doing this), dose, and fantasize. But I also felt more helpless, in a passive position, at times suffocated and cramped. Driving as a teen was a relief, freedom. Not as much at the mercy of being driven around where the adult wanted to go or take me.

Was the patient the baby, the child in the back trying to stop a bad thing from happening? Stop the primal scene, stop parental intercourse, the big crash, the bang, the disaster? I've often heard individuals say they were afraid their father was hurting mother when they heard bed and voice sounds at night. Freud did not make this material up. There is not just the pain of exclusion, but also fear the parents are injuring each other. A lot of movement heading for disaster.

It is as if in the dream a child is shouting, "Stop it! Stop it!" It is not just that they are not paying attention to me, that I'm left out, not part of the excitement or threat. It is that something awful will happen, an unspecified catastrophe, imaged in the dream by impending crash (real or imaginary). Or perhaps the child is trying to stop a crescendo of argument, fear of violence. A parental crash.

Or then again, perhaps there is trauma fear in the background. Something terrible is going to happen to me in face of looming parental power. The parent coming at me like a locomotive, perhaps to hit me, perhaps to boss me, a collision of wills or bodies or emotions. Fear of being overpowered and irrevocably damaged. Parental rape, emotional rape. I want it all to stop, to be still, before something awful happens – again, again.

Perhaps the dreamer portrays a catastrophe or sense of catastrophe that happened to him, or that he feared happened to him, imagined happened to him: the parents doing something awful to him or his body doing something awful to him or... The train wreck is going to happen, trauma happening. He can't stop it. How can I stop trauma? I'm helpless to stop trauma. Whatever way I try is not effective. They (parents, body, feelings) keep doing what they want, keep on doing bad things, and I keep feeling the bad things. I can't make the trauma stop. The train just keeps going, and there is going be a wreck, and I am going to be injured again. I can't stop them or it from injuring me.

Or perhaps a sense of trauma, impending catastrophe is more general. Impending catastrophe with a thousand faces. And the dream depicts a moment of helplessness, a sense that what we do in face of this generic sense does not do the trick. Our thoughts or actions may even substitute one bad event for another. Catastrophe without capacity to address it.

And if this catastrophe has to do with incapacity in face of our own emotional life? Emotions as catastrophic? Or lack of emotions as catastrophic. Helplessness in face of emotional catastrophe?

The child is helpless to stop the traumas from the parents or traumas from within. Whatever ways he tries do not work or do not work well enough. As Bion's patient's dream indicates, attempts to help oneself can lead to injury. Does one know where the pain is coming from and what it is or how to do something about it?

Bion points out that his patient's attempt to help was not successful, for one thing, because his arm behaved as if it were having a tantrum and fell onto the grass. It's not just that he is helpless, but a part of him behaved rebelliously. Something in him objected to his own course of action, part in revolt. One part feels and says, "I want to help." Another, disobedient aspect says, "No, I won't help. I don't want to help." It is as if the latter part says, "I want the crash to happen."

Aspects of the self do not want to conform with the executive ego. Be helpful. I don't want to help. A nasty element does not want to follow orders. But perhaps this "nasty" element has wisdom of its own, mind of its own. There is something to be said for not conforming to a delusional command or even an obviously ineffectual one. Still, the arm did not have to dramatize no by falling off. It could have merely refused to move, be paralyzed. It surely upped the ante with its antics.

A lot goes on in childhood – and all the rest of one's life – involving being good or being bad. The pleasure of being "bad" begins early, has a long history. It can be confusing when one learns ways bad can be good and good can be bad. There is a long cultural association of bad with individuality, breaking rules, going against the grain. For William Blake, Satan was a creative force in personality and culture, although for Blake, too, Jesus was creative imagination. Both sides or tendencies or forces contribute ("The Marriage of Heaven and Hell" 1975). Perhaps the arm revolts against a narrow form of mind. The arm knows better.

I remember once being supervised on a case in which a man complained of impotence. He got into feelings of threat and promise in a sexual situation. Something felt like it caved in out of compliance, that he was not really very interested. He did not really like the women he spoke of. He lacked feeling and real desire. My supervisor hearing this and more said, "His penis is smarter than he is." We could begin working with the deeper malaise and its intricacies rather than obsess about the presenting symptom. Much deeper incapacity marked his life. There are many ways to be "impotent."

If the dreamer's arm protested against the dream ego, it sure did it in a self-defeating way. To fall to the ground from a moving train, be severed from the body that gave it life, to end up lifeless – what kind of solution is that? It appears we have the kind of psychosomatic system that jeopardizes itself. It may be that we often cannot tell what furthers or harms our needs and growth. When I hear politicians speak about self-interest, usually as a means of getting their way with self-serving policies, I think – do they know what is in our interest? How?

There is a saying in English about "cutting off your nose to spite your face." We seem to have a psyche that hurts itself trying to help itself or further its self-interest. The dream may be trying to alert the patient – us too – about ways the psyche can work. I don't know if catching on to these ins and outs can stop them from happening or modulate them, but not catching on may be even worse.

A degree of force is part of what we do. We may force ourselves to get up in the morning to go to school, force ourselves to study for exams, to spend time on jobs we do not like or even hate, to stay in relationships that may not be as productive as we envisioned, and much else. We force ourselves and we rebel at the same time. Often the body pays a price. An aspect of the command center or executive ego may insist on certain acts which stress body and psyche. Shaping up to do well in this world creates tension, stresses tissue and mind. But so does not doing well.

Freud pointed out that just growing up stresses the psychosomatic system. Even standing up – one exerts oneself against gravitation. One becomes another kind of being. Growing has rewards, opportunities – but there are always prices to pay. One may not realize how much of oneself objects to what it is commanded to do and the pain that is chronically shunted, until it can be shunted no more.

Parts of the mind/body that we call self-defeating have a mind of their own. They don't want to or can't or won't simply follow orders from the top without repercussions. We speak of a helpful and unhelpful part of self, usually from the viewpoint of the command center. But a larger sense of personality as a whole may call these classifications into question. Unhelpful may be helpful in a larger sense, and helpful may be unhelpful, if it is occluding, treating other parts of the whole poorly.

Think of the so-called "negative twos." Or the child who does not want to get socialized, refuses to comply, or reacts against his own compliance. Or parts of us that tug against our false self-aspects. The nice part of personality might be baffled by its own explosiveness. A tug of war between control and impulse can make one ill. An executive part of personality can lay down the law, make plans that create unhappiness for the psyche as a whole. If psyche-soma is unhappy enough, organic problems may result, real effects and signifiers of helpless unhappiness. Too often will, power, desire move ahead without regard for strain caused. Breathing, digestion, skin often pay a price (or worse). Often what we feel impelled to do is imposed from without, but often it is forced from within. We are in tension with ourselves. We leave out a lot of ourselves. A lot of tensions, a lot of stress. Including inner stress among rebellious populations that make up personality. A conflict between psychic democracy and psychic tyrannies. Any part of personality can become tyrannical, any part can feel left out. Tensions between civil strife and peace.

Bion's patient was bewildered that such unexceptionable and good behavior, putting out his hand to stop the train, provoked such a hostile response. We are all vulnerable when we reach out to help. I might think the other hostile for tearing away, cutting off contact, as the arm did. But perhaps the other, the arm, was being independent. Perhaps I misconstrued that nature of my help and the seemingly recalcitrant response of the other responds to my misinterpretation. One may want to help but be wrong about what needs help or how to do it. There can be, too, conflict of wants. Saint Paul's: "I don't do what I want to do, and I do what I don't want to do." Sometimes a helping hand is like putting a hand up in front of a racing locomotive – the means to help inadequate to the wish.

Not having means sufficient to the task, I may feel my inner parts working against me and each other, not simply out of hostility or ill will, but also incapacity. Perhaps at a given time, unable to do better. Perhaps, too, my viewpoint gets in the way. I take my view for granted, but others within or without may see things otherwise.

I may feel my parts are working against me because of my small view of personality. I haven't taken my part-viewpoint into account. Perhaps my view is small compared to what is needed. It does not include enough of me. Why shouldn't they object – they want to be part of life too, part of a fuller life. I treat them as hostile rebels when they are seeking. They want admission to my life too. Maybe I leave them no choice but to swell my joints or taunt my guts, discontent with the cramped place they have left.

Maybe Bion's dream patient's arm was smart, and the patient stupid. Maybe the arm hoped for a larger view of reality and did not want to lend itself to an ill-conceived plan or impulse. I can hear the arm saying, "What stupid uses he puts me up to! How dumb a host person I belong to!" I think of another moment when Bion envisions a waving hand with the person saying, "I'm not waving. I'm drowning." An arm ever signaling distress. Drowning that never stops. A feared crash that never ends. Catastrophic anxiety as a driving force. No wonder the poor hand doesn't want to wave anymore, a tireless thankless task, ever signaling a catastrophe that never happens, that is always happening, a hand helpless to stop it, helpless to get help.

And what does this say about the help it gets from therapy? The therapist's helping hand? The help that never comes or doesn't make a difference. The arm as an impotent signifier, an impotent helper. A signifier of failed, impossible help.

Sometimes I think what if all soldiers of the world suddenly refuse to fight. Why should we sacrifice ourselves for the power dreams of leaders? Does such a drama in the social body, the body politic, have analogues in the psychic body, the physical body? Doesn't something in us feel it's worthless, stupid, cruel?

Bion felt the dream indicated that for this person attempts to be cooperative or creative were undermined by parts of his personality. No matter how good an intention, assuming it was good, it would suffer difficulties and possible defeat, thwarted by one's bodymind, tensions between creative and destructive tendencies. Bion particularly notes that a rewarding state of mind is denied by the arm's independence. I may want to help but not know how and fall into misguided attempts. I might want to enjoy a rewarding state which reality abuses. Reality may foil my wanting to feel good about myself and my actions. I want to feel good about myself but life and countertendencies slap my face, go against my picture of myself, challenging self-images. Another alternative: I am unable to accept, tolerate rewarding feelings.

But can one call an arm falling off in a dream reality? Possibly magnification of a part of feeling reality, the reality of feeling, a sense that my own being fails me. My being is not at one with itself. I imagine unity, but there is loss, surprise, trauma. The Bible speaks of one arm not knowing what the other is doing. Perhaps that applies to any set or subset of psycho-somatic systems.

There is something in me that would like to help. I am thinking about an individual I work with. Nothing I do is right. I can't find the spot. I think I find something useful, but it falls flat. My wish to help is put out of play, as if it is burdensome, misguided. It's almost as if the more I want to help, the angrier the person gets. At the same time I know that wishing to help, for some people, is experienced as a narcissistic need of the therapist. Therapist wanting to be appreciated like the patient's mother. Very far from Bion's recommendation of being without memory, expectation, understanding, desire, including the desire to help. For some, the desire to help can feel like an aggressive attack, an attempt to control, engulf, exploit. Help as a threat. The wish to help as a threat.

Amplifying Bion, we can go further. There is something in the personality that works against succeeding in an agreeable action. A destructive state substituted for an enriching state. A potentially pleasing state, like my helping a patient or Bion's patient achieving an agreeable state of affairs, is abruptly shattered. Instead of Bion's patient being a hero and applauded by his fellow passengers for saving their lives, the latter are annoyed by the extra inconvenience his lost arm causes. In one way or another, one might say the dreamer succeeds in stopping the train, not as he expected by a signal of danger, but to retrieve his arm.

In psychoanalysis we learn that sometimes feelings function as signals. Anxiety of a smaller kind can signify much larger internal dangers. Anxiety can be a hint to follow. So can fear or guilt or anger or shame. They can signal disasters that the personality could not "solve" but managed to grow over. Many scars are beneath our psychic skin. Sometimes if we can listen to our feeling signals, we can sense what is happening and not have to go through something worse. In Bion's patient's dream, a signal did not work and something more drastic was resorted to. The train stopped but the cost greater than merely a wave of the hand. It is important psychic work to keep our signal systems in good repair.

Still more deeply, there may be a force at work that prefers the crash to the avoidance of the crash. Like a child who can't stop a play session if not in tears. Or attractions that gravitate towards painful endings. A moment of good that veers towards bad, as if the psyche lacks a brake system, or is relatively helpless against a magnetic pull towards injury. Freud wrote about this as being stuck in trauma, repeating it over and over. It may also have to do with need or addiction or attraction to moments of devastation as a rock bottom touchstone with reality or with what feels real.

The push towards a wounding outcome can vary in intensity and result. It can be impacted by many factors. There is even such a thing as creative wounding. At the moment, though, I wish to say more about the compulsion to succeed, to keep on going in order to achieve a goal. A push that can be ruthless and relentless. I am thinking of a boy who was failing in school. His parents drove him to do better. He twisted himself out of shape, but even with tutors his mind rebelled against him, much as Bion's dreamer's arm.

He began getting illnesses that evaded diagnosis but which we debilitating. Anxiety in the family mounted as it grew, parental pressure increased. It was a vicious circle.

What compounded the situation was that the boy had been successful in school before this spiral began. The sharp decline and disability was unexpected (note that in all of Bion's clinical vignettes the turn from good to bad is sudden, often alarming; alarm seems to be part of it, whether as signal or reactive). The parents had a vision of the boy's excellent abilities and the good life ahead of him. If he continued in this downward course, what would happen to college, career? At this point, he might not even finish high school.

They went through myriads of reactions, mostly heightening the pressure, feeling he could snap out of this if he wanted. They could not grasp he was caught in something he could not control, even if now and then, for short periods, he seemed able to. Overall, he was caught in what seemed a compelling force. His mental spin and physical illness increased.

When I was consulted, I asked if there was anything the boy liked. "Horseback riding," they said. It was unlikely in his current condition he could get on a horse but I suggested they raise the question, maybe little by little. I thought of a case Masud Khan reported, advising a family to let their child do something physical, away from his school setting, take pressures off, a farm perhaps. Learning that the boy loved horses, Khan suggested taking a year off or whatever it took enjoying horses. In this case, follow the boy's love.

An idea like this was foreign to the parents. Not that they never had a flicker of such a thought. But any flicker was quickly shunted. The pull to stick to the main path was too strong. There are instances in which one can sacrifice a life in order to achieve a goal. Of course, in this situation by such a sacrifice no goal would be achieved but disability or death. How to revisualize one's child and oneself and life. Life is bigger than the sum of one's goals. Life may not go along with goals set for it.

In this case, the point was reached in which the boy was assured he would be off from school for a year or more. This was done with the school's knowledge and cooperation. He would spend the time following his love. Horses brought him back to life, engaged him in life.

One can speculate – did horses represent an animal nature that was getting flayed by societal pressures? Did it have to do with emotional spontaneity that was getting less and less room to breathe, dangerously close to being squeezed out of existence – physical and mental symptoms housing what was left of spontaneous promptings?

Along this line you might look at a chapter in *Contact with the Depths* (2011a), "Tears of Pain and Beauty," an account of a young man with repeated hospitalizations who became hospital free over the course of a long therapy in which vital feelings were supported.

It may be the boy who loved horses was heading for a great "train" crash. But in Bion's patient's dream, a crash did not happen. And thus in this boy's life, the ultimate crash was averted. It may be important to speak not only of a pull towards catastrophe, attraction to The Great Crash, but also a counter-part reality, the missed crash, a missed catastrophe.

Such considerations have relevance to a wide array of happenings, the temper tantrum in a supermarket, for example, or at home. Who is doing this? What is doing this? Often the child will express a want and the situation can be corrected. But other times nothing will do. Even if a want is expressed it cannot be satisfied. The need is coming from somewhere else, that not even the child knows about. Another self, you might say? Another part of the larger personality that is being left out of existence? Things happen quickly in the moment and what drives the child is likely left "unsolved" (if, indeed, a solution exists). One has to get through the situation at hand the best one can and leave reflection for later. How does one begin to address an underlying sense of helplessness in face of something one doesn't know?

In *Toxic Nourishment* (1999), I wrote about teenage suicide or suicide attempts. Often the latter came as a surprise to parents who thought everything was "good." A sudden alarm in some cases can come too late. On closer examination, signals of discontent were present but brushed aside, downplayed, pushed past. As if we have an inborn mechanism to ignore ourselves or those parts of ourselves that we fear will cause us trouble, slow us down, divert us from our ambitions and tasks. Perhaps still more deeply, we collude in pushing past what we cannot handle, what we lack capacity to work with. There are ways we feel helpless with ourselves, a helplessness with nowhere to go.

Not just pressures and stresses that are not being seen or addressed or taken seriously, stress between oneself and the world one lives in, stress between parts of oneself. Also inability to tune into, give space to, and care about a part inside that is saying no. Can one hear the no before it sinks a person? When, at what stage? And what if one is mistaken? For often one's situation may be bearable and, hopefully, in some or many, communicable. Still, it is important for individuals, families, society to become more attuned to a silent dimension inside in which we feel helpless before our helplessness.

I tend to feel if a person brings in a dream it is some kind of communication. What is the dream trying to tell us? Whether in or out of therapy, a dream is trying to tell the dreamer something, share something. Someone brought a dream he didn't understand. That's fine, the patient doesn't have to understand the dream and you don't either. But in some way you can communicate that a message as yet unknown is waiting, a sense of something important we may be able to approach someday. Something unknown is knocking at the door but we can't quite open it yet.

Suppose the dream is trying to communicate something negative and is now brought into therapy. You might sit and feel it, let it register, acknowledging something wants to be heard. Something in the person is trying to get through to the person using the therapist to mediate it. Depending on the feeling in the room you might communicate, whether verbally or non-verbally, something like "I hear your negative side." Or even, "I hear your negative side that wants to blow everything up, make a big mess of the whole business." More than what you say, an attitude of making room for communication comes through.

Another part of the negative (there are many) is to blow restrictions away, refusal to accept limit. One aspect can be to reach a boundless area of the self, a boundless field of feeling where restrictions are unacceptable. I feel trapped by my personality. I want to be free of myself. I want to be free of my personality. I don't want to be stuck with the kind of person I am. You might say that in Bion's patient's arm falling off dream the arm is protesting: my life is too restricted, limiting – this is not how I want to live. There has to be a better way and I want to try to find it. At the same time, there are parts of the self that want a fast and complete solution: "I want to blow the whole thing up," as if blowing it all up will reach absolute freedom, which in the life form we have is impossible. As I mentioned this morning, the life form we are imposes certain restrictions on us. There is a sense of limit we keep resisting and pushing against.

From another profile, experience teaches that we have a double sense of limit *and* boundlessness, dual states. In our life form there are ways boundlessness and limit go together, as Bion might say, a constant conjunction, part of a phenomenon I sometimes call a distinction-union structure. Aspects of dual structures fuse with and oppose each other, work with and against each other in varied ways. They exert pressures that affect our perception of external reality as well, e.g., divisions within and between social-political-religious systems as well as race and gender. Different parts of our being entangle, fight, dissociate, unite, nourish, and wound each other. Inner-outer tensions arise with regard to territory, economics, pride-humiliation-vanity, aesthetic and military power, domination-subjugation, knowledge. There are unknown forces that constitute our lives through tensions that perennially challenge us. We have an invisible domain of things that can and can't get along together, organismic, psychical, interpersonal, spiritual, chemical, political (inner as well as external politics). Look at the amazing relations we've had with our respiratory system, whole spiritual-organismic systems related to the experience of breathing.

Bion talks about the difficulties of common sense. In autism and various psychoses the senses may work against rather than with each, pulling each other apart rather than co-nourishing. Difficulty coordinating sensory input is not confined to psychosis. A lot depends on affective attitude, including whether one's emotional frame of reference is more combative or able to develop a better working relationship with one's capacities – a partnership rather than hostile control model, learning with and through experience rather than dogmatic, delusional omniscience. Nineteenth-century psychology had many portrayals of how different elements of personality would fight for more space in conscious attention, including the battle of ideas in a person, a kind of Darwinian struggle for survival and dominance (Gurwitsch, 1964). How do we learn to work with ourselves and our makeup is an evolutionary challenge that may take tens of thousands of years. Hopefully we will manage to keep learning how to work with ourselves and give ourselves more chances to live peacefully and fruitfully.

Later in this seminar, perhaps tomorrow, I hope to talk about Rabbi Nachman. Worlds of faith and dimensions of existence kept opening for him, heart after heart without end and he would try to help people who came to him experience the wonder of their existence more fully. In a way he reminds me of Carlos Castaneda's (1969) term "stopping the world" as a moment in transformational movement. To try to lessen the immediate pull of habits, he recommended meditating in a forest alone. Unfortunately, this often failed and led him to think that people need someone to fight with or, alone by oneself, one may tear oneself to pieces. Nevertheless, he recommended speaking from one's broken heart to God in ordinary language, a kind of psychoanalytic session with God, saying everything that hurts and wounds, the pain of existence. In order not to go crazy alone with oneself, we need to learn to fight with each other in better ways, less murderous ways.

Any questions, remarks, thoughts?

QUESTION 1: Earlier, you said that psychoanalysis is deeply beautiful. I'm hoping that you can elaborate little more on what that means.

RESPONSE 1: It may be my idiosyncrasy, but I feel very deep beauty sitting with someone with emotion that can't be tolerated or expressed. I'm thinking at the moment of someone feeling explosive and deadened at the same time. How does one help create a space not too big or small, an emotion-sensitive space that over time gives a person a chance for emotion to register and begin to be represented, have a voice, be recognized, develop an expressive language even for explosiveness and deadness. One thinks of poets through the ages developing poetic language for destruction. For love, creation, and positive beauty too. But opening gateways to what can't or dare not be said has its own kind of beauty, positive and negative. Psychoanalysis, for example, developed a language of wounds, so that in time states hard to deal with come out of hiding. In certain ways, psychoanalysis, poetry and religion provide language for so much inexpressible pain. Aspects of the work can be ugly, but it's a beautiful process enabling damage to be a little braver and come more fully into expressible being. We work at both ends of the spectrum, the cup runneth over with feeling and/or is empty and dry. For me, it's a beautiful part of life to help birth emotional possibility in face of immense damage (Eigen, 2014b).

Here is a quote from one of Bion's last seminars, *The Paris Seminar* (1978):

> It is very important to be aware that you may never be satisfied with your analytic career if you feel that you are restricted to what is narrowly called a 'scientific' approach. You will have to be able to have a chance of feeling that the interpretation you give is a beautiful one, or that you get a beautiful response from the patient. This aesthetic element of beauty makes a very difficult situation tolerable. It is so important to dare to think or feel whatever you do think or feel, never mind how un-scientific it is.

QUESTIONER 1: Thank you.

For the rest of the time today I'd like to say more about Bion's explosion and develop images and thoughts around it. My main concern is touching aspects of the human condition that need consideration, study, and elaboration. In one of his models, Bion (1970, Chapter 2; Eigen, 1998) uses Big Bang images for the birth of the psychic universe. Explosive processes are part of the psychic as well as physical universe. He posits a psychotic explosion in contrast with or in addition to explosive processes that help create the layering of psyche and consciousness generally. Beauty may be part of birth experiences (Eigen, 2014), but the latter also involve struggle and challenge. One can move between fusions, oppositions, and oscillations of beauty and agony. Bion is not claiming explosiveness characterizes all of our emotional life but is a significant factor as part of it.

Many philosophers remark on paradoxes of our nature. Pascal felt we were lower than angels, higher than animals, partly both and neither, something worse and perhaps better as well. Many observers of the human condition postulate areas of peace and turbulence. I sometimes ask if a person can find a point of peace amidst the turbulence and many point to the center of their chest (which corresponds to Tiferet, Beauty, the heart-center of the Kabbalah Tree of Life). Spiritual and healing disciplines develop ways to increase contact with a peace center as well as build tolerance of the turbulence.

Bion keenly observes that psyche has evolved faster than its capacity to digest and work with its products. This is a kind of amplification of Pascal noting that a disproportion characterizes human beings, e.g., multiple ways that we are ahead of and behind ourselves at the same time. Bion adds that our capacity to produce is far ahead of our capacity to digest and work with our mental-psychical products. Part of explosiveness is the birth and growth of psychic and mental life, including consciousness and self-awareness that the psychosomatic equipment can't support or is not able or ready to support well. There are ways we do not know what to do with ourselves. It is a growth challenge to bear the tension of having a mind with the range of thought and experience it has, let alone the range and depth of psychic agonies known and unknown.

Our minds are partly magnifying-minifying machines. We use the term "to blow up" to characterize certain "exaggerated" states. On the other side, I remember a patient who said she had a disappearing machine that made thoughts and feelings vanish. It saddened her that this attempt to minimize threat tended to zero out good feelings as well. We have a mind that under certain circumstances can take itself out, eliminate itself. Bion writes of maximum-minimum emotion, states that fuse, oscillate, oppose each other, turning up and turning down emotional volume and possibility. Our mind can maximize states and move towards zero at the same time, as well as develop maximizing-minimizing rhythms, a little akin to crescendo-decrescendo in music. Our mind can act like a plus-and-minus infinitizing machine blowing oneself up in both directions, intense overflow and null. Maximum emotion and minimum emotion. Emotion moving towards infinity and emotion moving towards zero.

In the examples I read earlier there is a kind of implicit explosion. For example, the man who gets half a cup of coffee from the waitress suddenly turns from good to bad state and explodes, "How could she! That ruined everything!" A change of state that runs through his emotional universe. In another example, someone throws a mug of beer in the patient's face. He manages to keep from screaming and tries to hold himself in good repair but everything is altered.

The arm falling off dream is another instance of sudden change of state linked to fear of catastrophe. It is as if the dreamer thinks losing an arm will avert greater disaster, pars pro toto, unconscious self-sacrificing to stop a crash. Throughout his work, Bion portrays heightened states psyche cannot tolerate – cataclysmic, unbearable pain that can lead to personality disintegration, breaking down, blowing up. In everyday life, all too often, catastrophic moments happen in miniature ways, including degrees and qualities of exploding to blot oneself out. It may sound odd to think of inner explosion as a form of self-numbing, but many forms of violence and numbing go together.

Following the psychotic Big Bang, Bion pictures personality breaking up and fragmenting, flying off into a kind of no-man's psychic space, parts of personality rushing faster and faster, farther away from each other and the point of origin into infinite, endless space where feelings thin out, diffuse, disperse. The more thoughts and feelings disperse, the less they can be thought or felt.

Again, maximum-minimum emotion. Unbearable explosion, agony that leads to loss of feeling. Another way Bion depicts loss of feeling following explosion is the image of surgical shock, when capillaries expand so much during surgery that blood flow thins to such an extent that one can bleed to death in one's own arteries. More broadly, it is important that your psychic space is not too big or small for you. If too small, you feel constricted. You might react with fight-flight to break out of it. On the other hand, if your space is too big you can't feel your impact. In either case, there is danger of losing self-feeling. Andre Green (1975) contrasts space too stuffed or empty with what he calls "well ventilated space."

More broadly, it is important to find a space that works for you, your particular relationship to space, your kind of space. When I was here before I talked to you about what I called "the Jim Henson Complex." Jim Henson was the inventor of *The Muppet Show* in America, a big children's TV series with lots of characters kids knew. Henson became very successful and at some point in his career began to sell rights to use his Muppets to industry. At one point he sold the rights of a Muppet especially close to him, Ernie, to Disney. Ernie was Henson's alter ego, a Muppet he most identified with, perhaps close to what Fairbairn called our central ego. Of course, the sale offered big profit. It so happened around the same time he had a cough he didn't pay attention to. After the negotiations and sale were over, he sought medical help too late. His lungs were congested, and they could not reverse it, and he died. It is my imaginary conception the space he was living in became so big he could not fill or feel it, but his lungs filled it instead. I know this may be crazy – it's OK to be crazy and try to use your craziness. His lungs substituted for psychosocial space and filled from within. It can be awful what unconscious processes can do. He was so successful but died of attack from within.

Tennessee Williams describes something similar but was conscious of it. After "A Street Car Named Desire" and his rise to success he began to lose his writing edge. He felt his creativity diminish and work became more stale. He no longer felt the sting that galvanized his creativity, life had become too easy. He thought of a possible way to make him feel the bite of life again by going to stay in Mexico without any money, just go as a poor person and undergo what fate would bring. But it was artificial and did not work.

I sometimes imagine that Shakespeare's success investing in real estate led to early retirement. He took what he made from writing and put it in real estate. One amazing play after another. When he felt he amassed enough money from investments he retired, left London for his country home, Stratford-upon-Avon, where he died after a couple of years at fifty-five. It is not necessarily a good thing not to feel the bite by life's pressure, life's edge.

How is it possible for one to undergo a psychotic explosion, agony that is an unbearable breaking point and at the same time not feel anything? An internal explosion that never stops, ripping one apart forever and at the same time not feel? Maximum agony and zero at the same time? Bion paints a remarkable picture of extreme states which I find very helpful as a model for fusion of maximum-minimum emotion. Infinity and zero can go back and forth in psychotic states, infinite and null states, hyper emotion and null emotion. For Bion both states are related to a primal catastrophe still ongoing in the personality. A catastrophic state that does not stop even after it is deadened or nulled.

Fifty years ago I was working with a so-called chronic schizophrenic man in a clinic. He was cherubic, always serene, impenetrable. He was very nice, a little chubby, smooth complexion. He said nothing bad about anyone. He lived with his parents and did some work, a narrow life surrounded by good thoughts and disposition. And periodically he would attack the milkman and had to be hospitalized. No one else – he would only get violent with the milkman. After hospitalization he would go back to being cherubic again. There is much more to say but here I am only noting explosiveness that was not usually felt but came out from time to time. I wish it had been possible to work with the explosive states themselves in well-dosed ways.

We all have psychotic states that we are aware of or not and go in and out of them. I am being generous saying we go out of them because they may be operative in some way outside of awareness. One can build empathic capacity to sit with unbearable-unfelt states and results of unbearable agonies that cannot be tolerated. You can sit with suppressed intensity and burnout, heightened intensity and turnoff. Over time you learn to make room for sensing painful emotion inside a person blowing the person up at the same time the latter may and may not feel it. You develop patience and even appreciation for the predicament a person is in because it cannot be represented. In time your patience and care may work as a background support enabling space to sense, represent, and begin to feel emotion that is usable. The blownup psyche is glimpsed in ways that allows psychic regeneration to begin its work. You somehow implicitly support lost capacity that has been environmentally eradicated or hasn't come to be. You can feel at least imaginatively, conjecturally, hypothetically and interact with pain this person must have gone through at the same time feeling, imagining the deadening process. Simply noting and feeling a person's predicament can go a long way.

Bion writes of a psychotic state as a kind of SOS signal, a kind of catastrophe signal that something awful is happening and no one can notice it, let alone tolerate it. You can begin to tolerate at least conjecturally and imaginatively the explosion and deadening processes that have no end. You provide an empathic background that over time begins to take residence in a person's psyche and makes a difference.

After Bion in Chapter 2, *Attention and Interpretation*, describes a psychic explosion he writes of two kinds of patients, A and B. A is someone whose psychic space blew up, pieces of personality flying off into immensity with nothing to hold on to, farther and faster away from the point of explosion and each other. Personality A, under trauma impact, gives up on itself, tries to get rid of itself. B is more able to tolerate existence of a space to project feelings into, or in Klein-Bion terms, tolerate projective-identification. Our focus here will be on A, who lacks a space to project feelings into, lacks an emotional container. You might say lost in "spacelessness."

Bion notes that A says he could not buy ice cream. Six months later he says he cannot even buy ice cream. Three days later he said it is too late to buy ice cream. There is no ice cream left. Two years later he supposes there is no ice cream. In the beginning there is ice cream he cannot access. It is there but he cannot get it. Good stuff does not exist for him. And then it was as if there never was ice cream. It vanished from the face of the earth. A movement from "ice cream is everywhere but I cannot get it" to "there is no such thing as ice cream." Bion then takes us through a few more steps until it reaches the point where ice cream becomes I scream. Life's sweetness or good taste is lost and a scream takes its place. And finally the scream dies out as well and there is no-scream. Both ice cream and scream die as links between personalities and self. A link to existence tends towards extinction.

I remember a moment when I refused to cry when my father hit me as a child. Did something die in me or get discovered or both? A birth and death at the same time in different ways? I won't cry. You sit on it. Hold it back. And gradually it begins to empty out. You numb it, kill yourself, but won't scream. Although I never stopped crying alone on my pillow. You cry yourself to sleep over the years.

Bion opens possibilities of seeing a lot of phases in the dying of a scream, e.g., from I won't to being unable to. And a poignant beauty of psychoanalysis is recovery of stages of your scream dying out and returning to life and its link with dramas of losing nourishment and sweetness.

I see we're out of time for today. Tomorrow I may talk about Kabbalah and Rabbi
Nachman and the missing X that is ineffably present.

Chapter 2
Day 2

Morning: heart, soul, and might

When I first saw Bion for sessions in New York he asked me if I knew the Kabbalah. I told him I knew it but didn't really *know* it. He said he felt the same way, he didn't really *know* it either. I've dipped in and out of Kabbalistic writings for forty or fifty years but wasn't a scholar. I was surprised he brought it up, seemingly out of the blue. He asked me particularly about the Zohar, a particular part of Kabbalah. Then we were quiet for a while and he said, "I use Kabbalah as a framework for psychoanalysis." I was startled and deeply interested. That remark stayed with me. I've thought about it a lot over the years. We met in 1977.

About two years ago, a colleague from New York University, co-founder of the New York University Contemplative Studies Project, asked me to do a workshop on Kabbalah and psychoanalysis. He had felt a kinship between aspects of my writings and work with Bion and certain central Kabbalah themes. Since that time I gave a series of workshops that became books (*Kabbalah and Psychoanalysis*, *A Felt Sense: More Explorations of Psychoanalysis and Kabbalah*, and *The Birth of Experience*).

As we go along, we will see if we can get some understanding of Bion saying that he used Kabbalah as a framework for psychoanalysis. Joseph Campbell years ago said he used the Hindu chakra framework in situating Freud and Jung. Perhaps there is some parallel in these studies.

The essence of Kabbalah is in one line of Torah: "You will love the Lord your God with all of your heart, with all of your soul and with all your might." In a way, that is the essence of the Torah, the Bible, and also the essence of Kabbalah. They have the same core. Love the Lord your God with all your heart, soul, and might. When I was a child I took that as a commandment. When I was little older, I took it as an invitation and challenge. And still much older began to think of the words not as commandment, invitation, or challenge but as a fact, a truth, a blueprint. You do in fact love God with all your heart, soul, and might. A field of love: I love You with all that is in me. A fact of existence, a deep fact of the human heart, part of the way we are made. I love You with all of me.

The Hebrew word for "Lord" is "Adonai" and that does not appear in this passage. The Hebrew word usually translated as Lord here is the "Tetragrammaton": YHVH, the capital letters Yod, Hey, Vov, Hey. No one knows how to pronounce it or knows its original meaning, the very name of God. "Lord" has been substituted for it. Bits of the Tetragrammaton appear in many places, like the pronounceable name of God, "Yah" – Hallelujah (Hallel-Jah): Praise God. My mind and being tends to associate the first letter of the unknown name, Y, as Yes. An Absolute Yes that in everyday reality undergoes many qualifications. I think of Molly Bloom in James Joyce's *Ulysses* crying Yes Yes Yes during a sex act and Thomas Carlyle affirming an Eternal Yea meditating on life and the universe. Simply the yes we have in common in our souls.

A well-known affirmation in the Jewish service begins with "Shema Yisrael Adonai Eloheinu Adonai Echad." Adonai – Lord – is a substitute for YHVH, the singular unknowable God. Eloheinu is a plural name for God, the many. Shema – listen, hear. Echad – one. Hear, O'Israel, the Lord your God is one. The one and the many are one. One could take liberties and say the plural is one and the one plural. All the many gods in the Bible and in the world are one. Can we speak of parts of one God, parts of God's essence? Are we referring to parts of our self, parts of our personality? A link, connection, between one and all?

One thinks of psychoanalysis as a "talking cure." But it is also a listening cure – if not cure a growth of process. Learning to listen. Learning to hear. I can't help saying that hear has ear in it and heart has hear in it. A psalm says, "Be still. Listen and know God."

Later rabbis assigned colors and numbers to letters of the Hebrew alphabet. They studied the values of words and names, for example, numerical values of God's names. Numerology became a deep interest, an attempt to unlock hidden meanings. The ancient Greeks used numbers to try to unlock hidden orders of the universe. The use of numbers to unlock mysteries of life, nature, and soul has a long history. This interest took new turns in modern science but many forms of numerological metaphors continue in their own right and intertwine with science as well.

Freud's confidant and cohort Wilhelm Fliess developed numerological systems depicting monthly biorhythms of patients. A particular dimension that interested Freud was the biorhythm between male and female aspects of personality, a biorhythm with associations in Kabbalistic numerology. Freud-Fliess worked with ascendency and recession of tendencies in different parts of a month. They tried to predict or develop a system for understanding the rise and fall of energy throughout the month, often associated with the menstrual cycle. One could easily imagine a lunar link as well. This aspect of Kabbalah was covert, not popularly disseminated, yet found its ways into psychoanalysis as a background for approaching male-female biorhythms. The notion of male-female aspects of personality was an enduring aspect of Freud's intuition, vision, and speculation.

Since antiquity, people have used letters and numbers to try to unlock and gain power over secrets of the universe. Some, too, experimented with letter-number permutations, not just for power but its own sake. At the same time, people explored spiritual meditation as a way to get closer to God, pathway to deeper union with God.

Kabbalah and psychoanalysis share a taste for hidden meanings. For Kabbalah, hidden meanings of Torah (Bible) bring one closer to God, catalysts for spiritual connection. For psychoanalysis, hidden meanings of the psyche. The category of the hidden permeates life. We try to decipher our existence. Love and dread of the unseen, unknown.

Over time Torah became more and more codified, resulting in an official book, a more or less unified Bible. Much was left out and elided pieces were collected into complementary, subsidiary, esoteric texts. The official texts themselves offered many starting points for deep as well as mad exploration, discovery of meaning never-ending. Plato spoke of divine madness that opened wings of poetry. There are also forms of madness that open gateways to spiritual joy, redemption, peace, and dread. Perhaps there is also psychoanalytic madness, a deepening love affair with the psyche opening tributaries of experience.

One example of a text left out of the official Bible is the Gospel of Thomas that teaches the kingdom of heaven both outside and within. Heaven everywhere potentially if you can find it, if you let it find you, a simple application of the teaching that there is no place without God. Kabbalah has at times seemed heretical in its sense of God everywhere, divine sparks awaiting care wherever you find yourself. In one sense, Kabbalah has never been codified but offers itself as an ongoing act of discovery. Attempts at unified viewpoints can be mined for living fragments. A little bit here and a little bit there, a kind of archipelago subverting and adding to any coherent unified official dogma.

In the Appendix of *Kabbalah and Psychoanalysis* (2012) you'll find a diagram of the Kabbalah Tree of Life, partly made up of spheres or circles noting human and divine capacities and functions. As you know the circle has a long history in human thought, mystical, mythical, mathematical, astronomical, psych-spiritual, aesthetic, poetic. We hear of circular movements of angels and meditations on the circle as image of time and eternity. We hear music of the spheres and I like to speak of music of the psyche. We live in a musical universe with a musical psyche.

Sphere is another word for dimensions, infinite dimensions that characterize our existence. The Tree of Life, then, emphasizes spheres of being, capacities of experience growing through a miraculous sense of aliveness. Adam and Eve's eating of the Tree of Knowledge (K) added additional, needed capacities that led to altered relationships to being. Now knowing filtered living and the search for life lost or unborn began.

Bion appealed to Faith (F) as an entrée to Being. And given the history of the circle he found his way to O as a notation for unknown ultimate reality, especially emotional reality in psychoanalysis. O filtered through F in contrast with K. Both are important and enter many relations with each other, antagonistic, opposed, nourishing, fused, interlinked, and dissociated myriad ways. There may be O-dimensions only faith can approach and ineffably touch. K offers and creates much but does not exhaust depths F in O opens. Bion links F with intuition. I am tempted to say intuition of the holy, a sense of the sacred. But intuition of reality can also be dreadful, as Saint Paul confessed. Whether peaceful or turbulent, Bion writes of an intuitive sense of atonement (at-one-ment) arising, opening (O) through F, a dimension of at-onement with oneself, life, existence.

When I work with people my intuition tells me what is appropriate. Lines of interest have many tributaries. I might suggest focusing on a word, image, thought, or sensation that touches a particular emotional nerve. Biblical images have special power but any part of life one is drawn to can feed meditation. Just sit with it, be with it. Don't force it this way or that. I'm reminded of the Zen master who told an artist to paint a dragon on a temple wall. The artist objected that he had never seen a dragon. The Zen master replied, "Sit here until you do. Sit here and see." And six months later the artist saw the dragon to paint on the temple wall. Just sitting with something, looking, feeling, tasting, smelling. Sitting and letting it play. Sitting with what you are drawn to or what is drawn to you. And if someone says, "Nothing is happening," I might ask, "What kind of nothing?" There are so many qualities of nothing. Nothing is inexhaustible.

I began speaking of an essence of Kabbalah and would like to return to it: Love God with all your heart and soul and might. Later, mind was added. What can "all" mean? Is there an all in human life, or are all states mixed? Ah, look how funny, I just said "all." Different rabbis have different interpretations. Yet there appears to be general agreement that all includes good and evil inclinations. Even our evil inclination is enjoined to love God. Nothing is exempted. Nothing is outside this love of God. Our hate loves God.

I would like to take a little detour to bring out aspects of love that is "all," that grows from and expresses our whole being. I wish to speak about the origins of the Zohar and say something about Rabbi Akiva. The Zohar became one of the most important mystical Kabbalistic texts, some would say the most important, one that Bion mentioned. He may have been thinking about the Zohar when he said to me, "I use the Kabbalah as a framework for psychoanalysis." But there are many Kabbalistic texts from many ages, authors, themes. Zohar is one of the landmarks. It was thought by many that Rabbi Shimon bar Yochai wrote it while he and his son were hiding from the Romans, roughly 288 CE. Roman law ordered that Jews be killed – usually by crucifixion or burning – if found practicing their faith. Shimon and his son escaped to a cave where they studied Torah, meditating on its deeper secrets for thirteen years. It was in this intense concentration that the basic blueprint of the Zohar was said to emerge. Zohar means radiance, splendor, illumination, glow. The glow that you see in paintings of saints with halos around them, expressions of the holy glow within. Shimon bar Yochai was thought to create-discover an amazing holy text filled with mysteries while in hiding, a text disseminated over time.

However, scholars conclude that the Zohar was written by Moses de Leon (1240–1305) in Spain. Rabbi Shimon bar Yochai was one of the main characters of the Zohar so it could easily be thought that Rabbi Shimon wrote it. But scholars believe it was Moses de Leon using Shimon bar Yochai as a character, much like Chuang-Tzu used Confucius or Lao Tzu as characters, attributing to them mixtures of what they may have said and what he made up. Chuang-Tzu added his own tone, spirit, inventions that were powerful expressions of life's spiritual imagination. Some say Moses de Leon channeled Shimon bar Yochai in acts of spiritual creation. Whatever the process, Moses de Leon's words inspire many seekers today and Wilfred Bion was one of them.

There are religious groups today that still think Shimon bar Yochai wrote the Zohar and made a holiday commemorating the day of his death. Whether the writer of the Zohar or not, he was one of the people who kept the spirit of his faith alive during the time of persecution. He was, you might say, part of a spiritual underground. Some say Akiva was Shimon's teacher, a spiritual link between them, a kind of intensive care of spiritual life. My feeling is they go on teaching each other and us and keep on doing so, soul to soul.

Akiva (50–135 CE) was a "throne" mystic, in part following Ezekiel's imagery in which an inner vehicle (Ezekiel's chariot) links soul to divinity (God's throne). The imagery is figurative, expressing aspects of spiritual experience, a soul journey ever touching God. In this case stillness and movement are indistinguishable.

Akiva may well be my favorite early rabbi. Let me tell you some Akiva stories I've heard since childhood. Four men enter the garden. It could be the Garden of Eden but could also be the Kabbalah, place of secret wisdom. One man went crazy, one killed himself, one became a heretic, and the fourth, Rabbi Akiva, emerged glowing. Whatever we call the garden is in all of us and we can relate to it and it to us many ways. The Akiva in us can go anywhere in the depths and emerge aglow. Other aspects of our being may have a harder time and fail to prosper or we may enrich ourselves by encountering each of them and exploring states and tendencies that are part of our makeup, mixtures of dreads and joys.

In the mystical garden we encounter our psychotic core, the madness that is part of our beings. We are not only mad and not only sane. From the point of view of spirituality and depth psychology, we have the chance to assimilate some of our madness or, at least, get the feel of working with it so that bits of its energy add to life's riches. We can grow through contact with the depths. Contact that can illuminate and/or madden. A job is to get the feel of it, sense how to work with it so that life grows with it.

Here is a little story from Akiva's childhood I've known since mine. Akiva was illiterate until his forties, but that's another story. As a boy he was sitting in the back of the prayer house. Since he didn't know the language, couldn't read or write, didn't know the prayers, he sat in back saying over and over the little bit he knew, aleph, bet, dalet, gimmel...the Hebrew alphabet, what we call the a-b-c's. He poured himself into each letter with utter devotion, all his heart, soul, might, all his Godly feelings. The rabbi leading the prayers began to notice a glow coming from the back where Akiva was saying the aleph-bet. The congregation looked around and saw the glow emanating from the little boy.

This holy state of being is often called *kavanah,* a Hebrew word meaning intention or better here, a heart-state, Akiva's soul-state lighting the prayer house. The cup runneth over with devotional spirit. It is a story that influenced my life. Don't look simply at what you can't do but pour yourself into what you *can*. Akiva lacked the official tools but used what he had with his whole being. Use whatever you have to the extent you can. Live with all you have even if it is a little. We are little bits of something greater but precious little bits. Each little bit is a doorway to immensity, William Blake's infinity in a grain of sand. Akiva became the glow of prayer itself. The little we have may not be much but it can glow.

When Akiva was older he had many followers although Jews had to practice in secrecy. Some of his followers organized attacks against the Romans although many were martyred. They were crushed and regrouped often at a loss. Somewhere along the line, the Romans captured Akiva, an elder by this time (he may have lived to 85). They crucified him and set fire to the cross at the same time. And as if crucifixion-burning was not enough, they peeled his skin off. In this final agony he felt and thanked God saying, "In all my life I loved you with all my heart and soul. And now I have the chance to love you with all my might, all that I am, all that I possess." All of me, my whole being. Apparently he implicitly had felt something lacking in his love that he felt completed on his execution. A grisly, merciless execution. He died in perfect faith of giving everything.

Now who can give everything? If you can't, then give what you can give. That might be as close as you can go. Find what you can give and pour your everything into that. Whatever you can give will have to approximate giving everything. Perhaps in some miraculous way, giving what you can becomes the same as everything.

We will take a break and when we come back I will fast forward to 1300s, 1500s, and 1800s, if time allows.

QUESTION: My question is related to content from yesterday regarding the space that fits – not too big, not too small. You gave some examples in which the space suddenly became too large and eventually resulted in death. So the question is about the relation between expansion of space and burning out in the sense that someone can use all their resources, burn out and die.

RESPONSE: It is all very individual. What you describe may happen with some people. There are many possibilities. It is also possible the more you use yourself, the more there is to use. The more you look into something, the more you see. Maybe some people use themselves up and die. But it is also possible the more you go into something, the more you *can* go into it, more keeps opening. The psyche never stops and possibilities keep unfolding.

In a way, Freud said our character kills us, uses us up. We all die. Buddha died at eighty. One of the last things he reportedly told his pupils, "Be a lamp unto yourselves." Some think he could have gone on forever but even so, it may be states and realities he pointed to go on forever or, at least, offer themselves for further exploration, use, aid. What he gave us or, as Socrates might say, midwifed, continues opening.

Nevertheless, what you say are words to the wise. Try to develop a sense of balance, how much *you* can take, what will work for you and what may harm, partly a matter of trial and error, learning from experience, sensing. In this, "Be a lamp unto yourself."

Any other questions, thoughts, comments?

If not, I'll dip into 13th–14th centuries, the time of Moses de Leon, a Spanish mystic who wrote the Zohar. He wrote in a kind of Aramaic that might have been used in the time Shimon bar Yochai lived. Moses de Leon said he found an old manuscript by Shimon bar Yochai the latter buried, including the Zohar and other writings. Moses de Leon disseminated the idea that the Zohar which he presented to the world was authored by Shimon bar Yochai. When Moses de Leon died scholars came to see the original manuscript Moses claimed was Shimon's writing. "Here it is," Moses' wife said. "You can look at it. He made it all up." There was no such ancient manuscript.

Why did he make it look like Shimon bar Yochai wrote it? Why didn't he just publish it as an invention of his own genius? His wife said he told her if he publishes under his own name, who would read it? It would go unnoticed. If he publishes it as a finding from antiquity by the great Shimon bar Yochai, people will take it seriously, pay attention, and study it.

And they did pay attention. This "finding" supposedly written by Shimon bar Yochai in the second century became a basic mystical text for later Jewish mystics, significantly elaborated in the 16th through19th centuries and currently studied as inspiration for further opening of experiencing and thought. There are many Zohar study groups.

Someone asked me during the break if the Kabbalah is a unified book? So let me repeat: It is not a single book like the Bible but many scattered fragments and texts over time. The Zohar itself is five or twelve volumes depending on the English translation, a series of adventures of spiritual imagination. You might call it a giant fragment among many fragments, pieces that touched the human spirit over hundreds of years. People studied its visions and words as a road to deeper God-contact. It builds on many discoveries from the Torah, finding deep spiritual meanings that become vehicles for connecting with God. Themes drawn from 3,000 years of oral and written transmission touch souls today and continue to be amplified, sources of creative experience. There are vast roots of mystical writings with touchstone constellations that stimulate us this moment.

The next figure I want to talk about is Isaac Luria (1534–1572), born in Jerusalem after the Spanish Expulsion. He was a profound student of the Zohar and disseminated new teachings through his talks. He wrote very little but a devoted student, Chaim Vital, organized and published his talks. It is said that Vital wrote down every word Luria spoke. If you are writing down what someone says you tend to reshape it and it may be more accurate to speak of Luria-Vital than either alone.

Luria is someone Bion speaks about, quoting Gershom Scholem's writings on kabbalistic teachings. Bion mentions Luria and Jesus as examples of what he calls Mystic or Genius dimensions of mind-spirit, visionaries who breakthrough the Establishment (Bion, 1970). In their cases, both died young. It is a difficult task to bring together Mystic-Establishment so that co-nourishing rather than destructive relations can grow.

Luria moved to Safed, a small mountain town where he hoped to find opportunity to study, meditate, and teach with less friction and continue to grow. On the same trip I visited Rabbi Akiva's grave in Galilee and Rabbi Luria's haunts in Safed, a mystical duo spanning nearly 1,500 years. I can't guarantee it, but I may have prayed in a shul Luria taught at and for me the vibrations were profound. One speaks of the spirit of a place and one may feel soul-to-soul transmission.

Safed was a seed of Jewish mysticism in the 16th century, a blossoming of Jewish mysticism for that time. It was a fecund birthplace of texts on Jewish law and mystical encounter. Both combined in Safed, quite a wedding. In one of Bion's images he speaks of the Big Bang of the psyche. Luria begins with God as everything and all and pictures God pulling back, contracting, to make room for the universe and living beings. I've often imagined God contracting as a kind of bow. Drawing and elaborating on earlier sources, Luria depicts divine energy channeling through creative vehicles called sephirot, emanations, attributes that parallel human capacities (e.g., wisdom, understanding, knowing, judging, compassion). Ten are usually represented in the Kabbalah Tree of Life but there are more beyond them and their combinations. Through the work of the vehicles of creation, time, and space, and the world as we know it emerges in all its specificity.

In some way one can speak of a fit or resonance between godly and human capacities and also difference, a gap or break between them at the same time. Difference and resonance go together in human experience, fit-and-break a basic structure or rhythm. You can view the Sephirot as a medium that channels God-energy. God creates the instrument that transmits energies to mediate between Himself and what He is creating. The Sephirot act as links between realms, while there is also a sense of an unknown Ineffable beyond image and conception.

Bion's grid has a certain parallel with the sephirot in that it diagrams mental-psychical dimensions that one may use to try to situate materials in sessions. However, not all psychical functions reach the grid and can be noted by it. Much goes on off the grid we do not or cannot know about. Similarly, the Sephirotic Tree is part of a larger unknown reality.

The Sephirotic Tree can be represented as a tripartite kind of cross, a vertical line down the middle with three horizontal lines/branches across. The sephirot express different capacities, functions, processes, dimensions, spheres of existence, attributes of godly emanations in the human sphere, possible flows, and organizations of godly energy that we share in our particular ways. Sometimes it is diagrammed as a lightning flash coming from above and going through all the pathways. There are various ways of trying to give expression to a basic intuition or vision or ineffable sense.

Although the sephirot are godly emanations manifesting as human capacities we speak of the unknown God beyond the tree or grid, impossible to circumscribe by capacities. This "off" the grid reality we call Ein Sof which means without limit, boundless, Infinite of Infinites, the God that can't be conceptualized, imaged, circumscribed by representations. In this context that God we call Yahweh, the God of creation, the God named "I am what I am or what I will be" is a kind of "lower" manifestation of the godly essence expressed through Ein Sof.

Yet we have a God-sensation, a faith-sense. Bion tries to give expression to such a sense when he states that the fundamental psychic reality is infinity that no language can get anywhere near describing, not even artistic, religious, or literary language. In semi-practical terms, Bion speaks of unknown emotional reality informing therapy sessions and develops a notation, F in O, faith in unknown transformational realities, particularly emotional realities. He calls faith the psychoanalytic attitude, openness to the unknown and mediating processes. Although we cannot know O, unknown ultimate reality, it impacts us and we respond, impact and response, ongoing. A mystical dimension in human life bears witness to "something" indescribable, ineffable, unimaginable that Bion sometimes calls "no-thing."

Chuang-Tzu (1964), a purported atheist, speaks as if there is a mysterious creator that can't be found anywhere, no form, yet seems to influence our lives and goes on forming us throughout our lifetimes. Something formless giving rise to so many forms. Chuang-Tzu humorously talked about being reincarnated as a pig's liver or some other wildly ludicrous form. Many Kabbalists share a view that spirit incarnates in varied ways over time. For example, King David's soul will someday be reincarnated in the Messiah. Ein Sof is beyond conception, but Bion might say we approach mystery through faith, including impact and faith-full response; some say felt call and response, unknown intimacy. An unknown that could be the most intimate fact of our lives. How can this unknown x be the most intimate fact of felt existence?

The ultimate unknown creative force, nameless, imageless one might liken to Buddhism's sunyata or no-thing emanates through the spheres of the sephirot, the capacities that make up the Kabbalah Tree of Life. Marion Milner (Eigen, 1983) speaks of creative emptiness in an attempt to touch an important moment of experience which has similarities to Bion's F in O, faith in unknown, ultimate reality. As mentioned above, Bion calls Faith the psychoanalytic attitude, a radical openness he tries to depict as being without memory, expectation, understanding, or desire.

There are parallels between the sephirot and yoga chakras. Both are represented in a kind of vertical picture situating various centers of energy and capacities using the human body as a frame, reality, and metaphor. The top point is Keter or crown, a kind of point of entry for divine emanations that support and in-form the universe, potential for all content but not bound by content, often depicted as no-thing, hidden light. God gives birth to the world through creative emanation, what we might call creative heart energy. The spinal column as an energy conductor is in kundalini yoga. The upright posture is a kind of model for vertical flows with associated images of heaven above, earth below, head above, heart, genitals, legs below. Across the "vertical line" are sets of functions on either side and middle. Mystical visions and networks make use of above-below, side-to-side, in-out, and beyond.

Divine transmissions through Keter flow to Chochma, the latter likened to a divine flash associated with wisdom. The capacity, attribute, emanation called Chochma (literally "potential to be") is situated on the tree below Keter at the head of the upper right branch. One might liken it to an insight seeing the whole of things, a kind of "Wow, I see it all at once." Mozart spoke about an intuitive flash in which he would "see" a symphony all at once. An instantaneous "seeing" (and "hearing"?) the symphony calling for birth, needing to work out the actual notes and details through the labor of other capacities.

From Chochma divine energy-emanation flows to Bina, understanding, directly opposite Chochma on the left side of the tree. The conjunction of chochma and bina gives rise to Da'at, knowledge, in the middle between them. Da'at is not technically regarded a sephira but a space is given to it, although often not written. A kind of empty space akin to the neck chakra linking head and body, reserved for all the ways the sephirot can combine to yield different kinds of knowledge.

Sometimes, I imagine the crown (unknowable opening) seeding wisdom, seeding understanding and knowledge. Seed-flash feeding us as we make poems, scientific discoveries, babies of many kinds. It is said these transmutations of energy have a direct connection with Ein Sof, including a kind of knowing that can bypass chochma and bina, an invisible direct link of the capacity to know with Ein Sof, God-capacities, human capacities mirroring each other, resonating, vibrating. At the moment, can't help thinking of current research on mirror neurons and Schreber (Eigen, 1986) feeling a mirror neuron connection with God.

Wisdom, understanding, and knowledge, generally associated with intellectual functioning, associated symbolically with the head, although not strictly confined there (Job to God: Now I know You in my flesh; or the biblical knowing associated with sexual intercourse).

The next level of the tree is associated with feeling, a more emotional level. Chesed (mercy, loving kindness) on the right side of the branch, Gevurah (judgment, severity, fear, discipline, evaluation) on the left. One may try to balance the two, too much or too little of one or the other. And between them in the middle is Tiferet, beauty. One can meditate on the beauty that comes from the mating of judgment and mercy. Beauty is the heart-center of the tree radiating in all directions.

The third set of branches has Netzach on the right and Hod on the left. Netzach is called victory, Hod splendor. Among Netzach's many meanings and functions is the capacity to overcome obstacles, whether inner or outer. It includes a kind of will to act and motivates the self to do something, e.g., struggle to add more loving kindness in self and world, active intention, and effort to spread goodness. Hod is more related to surrender, prayer, openness to the fullness of being, often receptive to the efforts of Netzach, the two combining for a more comprehensive context or frame, Hod adding deep sincerity to Netzach's will and muscle. Netzach as depicted as the right leg and Hod the left, as Chesed is the right arm, and Gevura the left. With netzach-hod we enter means-end and cause-effect relationships at work in the world, combining strength and gratitude.

Perhaps you will not be surprised to learn that in the middle of netzach and hod is Yesod, genitals, called Foundation. A basic reference is to male-female procreative organs, referring to generativity on many levels, including the continuation of humankind. One thinks of the biblical encouragement to be fruitful, which may mean a fruitful life, fecund existence as well as literal children. Freud would be happy with the important role sexual energy plays in the Tree of Life, combining sexual-aggressive tendencies.

The tenth sephira is Malchut, in the center of the tree under yesod. It is called Kingdom and refers to our life here on earth as gateway to heaven, with particular emphasis on growth of self-expression in thought, speech, and action, including and perhaps especially soul-work. It is a wonderful link that soul-work is also associated with leg-work, as Malchut receives energy directly from the leg trio – netzach-hod-yesod. The holiest prayers in the service are said standing and sometimes bowing. Even in common language we speak of a work of art or literature as having legs, continued interest and movement and possibly ongoing soul-creation. Harold Bloom (1975, 1998) gives a secular example of this process when he calls Shakespeare a god who created the human as we know it, a breakthrough of sensibility we are still mining today. What a profound love of creativity he had and shared and it is no accident he also wrote a book about the kabbalah.

We will take a lunch break now but I'd like to mention that the last four sephirot couldn't take the pressure and intensity of divine energy and broke in the process of creation. The sephirot were "tools" or vehicles God used in the creation of the world and some shattered in the process. The intensity of creativity and emotional life – a boon, danger, challenge.

* * *

Afternoon: hidden sparks

Sometimes it is helpful to think about a structure of the sephirot in terms of Jung's four functions: intuition, thinking, feeling, and sensation. As divine energy emanated through the channels of creation, the lower channels shattered, unable to take the full intensity of the flow. The tenth sephira, Malkut, foundation, birth of the kingdom of God on earth is often identified with the Shekina, God's feminine side and holy presence, something like the Holy Spirit in Christianity. God's presence on earth and in you. A painting I saw by Anselm Kiefer depicted the Shekina's garment as torn, expressing the theme of shatter, breakage.

Rabbi Luria was born in Israel but his family was exiled from Spain. A theme of not belonging mixed with belonging, shattered vessels that could not take life, yet endured in search of wholeness, compromise, ways to live. It is like saying God's presence broke under the impact of His own creative energy and that shatter and brokenness is part of life. In a way, Kabbalah is a response to trauma at the same time it is a profound affirmation of the human spirit and Divine Spirit as well.

There is deep resonance between Bion's work and Kabbalah. Bion is ultra-sensitive to psychic catastrophe, a psyche that can't take its own explosive intensity and tries to get rid of itself at the same time it tries to learn how to work with itself. It is challenged to build capacity for psychic work (Eigen, 2018). One is challenged to support the growth of the psyche so it can begin to work with its own intensity and multiple capacities.

Lurianic Kabbalah insists it is our calling to repair the broken pieces of creation, which includes and emphasizes the vehicles and powers of creation. Wherever we are there are hidden sparks to mine, holy sparks that flew everywhere in the shatter. Soul sparks seeking re-unification, repair, sustenance so they can, in turn, sustain us. World-self-God repair is part of our mission. Wherever you find yourself there is a spark only you can help set free, continuing and furthering possibilities of creation. Every moment you are up to it awaits your creative partnership.

I'm thinking now of some moments when I was here in 2007, the last case of the day (Eigen, 2010). A theme in the patient's life was brokenness and we shared the brokenness of our lives together, paradoxical moments of beauty. In the depths of the sharing one feels how beautiful this work can be. Shatter and brokenness is a common theme in Kabbalah and Bion and many mythic narratives. Creativity that breaks vessels that mediate it, intensity too great for the psyche to take. We are in the position of having to tolerate the intolerable bits at a time. Pain so great that it may provoke murder-suicide as a way to try to end it.

What can we do with the pain of life? Pain that shatters frames and containers that try to modulate it. Yet we keep trying, partners in pain, evacuating, muting, handling, creatively using. Bion, too, speaks of suffering joy, building capacity to tolerate experience a little better, a little more. In what ways can you tolerate yourself and tolerate working with yourself? Can you find value in emphasizing what you can do and not be done in by what you can't? In extremis, Bion speaks of a negative as well as positive grid. The latter tries to build on and with experience, take life farther. The former works in reverse, undoing, nulling, a destructive force that feeds on itself. And we? We are in the middle rolling back and forth and with luck, grace, perseverance, faith dimensions keep opening and opening us.

I'd like to move on to a structure that underlies a lot of human experiencing. In *The Psychotic Core* (1986, 2018) I write of a distinction-union structure, a kind of DNA/RNA of experience. It is not necessarily a good name and there may be better ones. But I needed some way to point to a double thread that makes up our lives, distinction dimensions and union dimensions. A double thread running through culture, history, mystical, and everyday experience: a sense of being separate and connected. I view this double thread as a single structure made up of varying sub-structures.

Distinction-union can be co-nourishing, oppositional, fused, or work on parallel tracks. But no moment of experience is entirely without either. The term tries to touch a reality that brings together rather than splits binaries, so that even splits are part of larger linking processes. In light of the overall structure, one against or fused, or working with the other are currents supplying something necessary for our lives. So very often we try to split one tendency from the other, e.g., this against that, yet both sides contribute to the color of life and work we need to do. Sometimes opposition is part of a larger partnership in growth processes. We need many tendencies to aid adaptation, survival, and transcendence. Conflict is part of growth in capacity to relate to complexities that make us up.

It is common to find opposition as part of linking structures in couples. No need to choose between opposition-fusion if we see them as part of larger distinction-union movements. Reversal of positions sometimes seems like the in-and-out of breathing. It's not simply a matter of this versus that but how they function as parts of a larger field of experience. Many capacities call for development but we cannot favor all of them in the limited time we have. What works for us in a particular phase of life is a semi-open structure subject to development.

In cinema and literature difference tendencies are divided up between characters. A person who tends to be more separate will run into x difficulties while a more fused person runs into y difficulties. In the course of the story each will have to develop some of the other side or new links with the other. Distinction and union individuals may clash, be attracted or repelled by each other, undergo transformations making room for both sides to exist and better partner with life. There may even be a hint of reversal, the aloof one becoming closer and the closer becoming more separate. Possibilities are myriad with varied distributions of clinging, detachment, longing, pushing away.

Basic relational patterns are memorialized in art but you see them happening in everyday life as a matter of course. We speak of dramas between two sides of personalities, individuals, groups, or nations but two is a stand-in for the play of multiplicity in any unit of being. Not two tendencies but triple, quadruple, and more than one can perceive at a single glance. Which of the whirling pool of possibilities, in what combinations and ways, are important for you to develop in your life? There is no question that selections must be made, although so often they let you know or give you hints by the way they touch your felt being. No one tendency can work alone. Counterparts and multiplicity are necessary for work to be done.

Working together even in opposition is a crucial capacity to keep developing, including working together with yourself and your self-oppositions. There are ways diverse tendencies can correct each other. Bion said that one of the advantages of having both love and hate is that you can see the world from each viewpoint, the two together with others testing reality. Therapy is like a house with many rooms that welcome a lot of visitors. It gives the person a chance to meet a diversity of tendencies and let them have a say and make their contribution.

A deep example of distinction-union structure in the Holy Trinity, the Father, Holy Spirit, and Son, all parts of the godhead, one God, yet three distinct personalities. One yet three, three yet One, is a profound expression of sides of human nature that separates-unifies, one yet many, many yet one. Our sense of time also shares this tri-un structure, present, past, future inextricably united yet distinct. This is an organizing experiential tendency that runs through our lives and a way we experience time.

What may seem like a surprising result of this one-yet-many structure is a single-double sense of inclusion-exclusion. One can emphasize the inclusive oneness and/or one's singleness, which can lead to a sense of exclusion, something left out. What is the distinction side doing? What is the union side doing? Wherever you find yourself there is another side, something left out, something other or more. This can make for loneliness but it can also yield a measure of freedom. What a person is talking about may be one thing, but there is much connected with it that is not being said or can't be said, always another side, another string to pull.

In psychoanalysis one way a distinction-union structure plays out is Freud's emphasis on separation-identification – separate yet identified with selected others, ideologies, national agendas. For example, separation one pole, identification with a leader another. We can grow through identifications and lose ourselves in them depending on context and function. A variation of this capacity is Walt Whitman saying, "Do I contradict myself? Very well then I contradict myself. I contain multitudes." He could have written, "I am multitudes" to add emphasis to our multiplicity, one yet many. There are ways individuals can identify with anything and everything and also remain separate.

Henry Elkin (1972) notes that communion has both dimensions: co-union. A union of distinct beings. Matte-Blanco (1975, 1978) writes of two forms of thinking, two modes of being, symmetrical-asymmetrical. Asymmetrical emphasizes difference: you are not me, I am not you. A jack of spades is not a jack of hearts. There is a tendency to separate, distinguish, and make distinctions on many levels. A semi-logical example of symmetrical thinking-experiencing is the statement, "All mothers are women." Here objects in a set have certain elements in common. For the psyche experiencing-thinking symmetrically prone to reversal it may also be the case that "All women are mothers." In such an instance everything in a class shares an identity, the same in some way. While a moment may emphasize symmetrical or asymmetrical experiencing, both are present, at once one and the same and different. A patient who overly sees all women as mothers and acts accordingly may need help balancing perspective, so that distinction-union poles work more positively together. Of course, the balance between symmetrical-asymmetrical dimensions shifts throughout experience but catching on to this dual play can help one grow.

In extreme, the symmetrical tends towards everything is everything else, the asymmetrical everything is different, and nothing is everything else. We can view the world both ways at the same time and/or alternate, one in the foreground, the other background. The symmetrical tends towards infinity, the asymmetrical towards discrete finitude. Matte-Blanco proposes that the unconscious works symmetrically, consciousness asymmetrically. He posits multiple levels/dimensions of both conscious and unconscious experience and work. The deeper the unconscious level, the more symmetrical and the more conscious, the more asymmetry. The deeper, the closer to infinity, everything is one, everything is everything, while the more developed consciousness, the more differences. Every psychic act is made up of both in complex ways.

Bion may have been reading Matte-Blanco when he wrote, "The fundamental reality is 'infinity', the unknown, the situation for which there is no language – not even one borrowed by the artist or the religious – which gets anywhere near to describing it (1992, p. 373)." He also was moved by kabbalah readings which included references to *Ein Sof*, the unknown infinite beyond name and representations. One could add writings drawn from many sources, e.g., Bion's references to Saint John of the Cross, the latter's dark night of the senses. As if such writings converge in a moment or point that mediates a depth that touches all depths. Allies from many quarters who point to realities space-time causal thinking may obscure yet also can open.

A letter I received from Matte-Blanco many years ago spoke about the importance of creative clinical description to convey a sense of psychic complexities, interplay of multiple realities, dimensions, and how impoverished so much professional writing seemed to be. We spoke of Bion and Meltzer (1973) among those who risked what Bion called a "Genius" or "Messiah" element of personality in contrast with the "Establishment" and difficulties inherent in container-contained relationships. Bergson, too, depicted creative-conservative dialectic and Emerson appears to inform aspects of Bion's sense of unknown Creative Power that permeates existence, as does Wordsworth's "intimations of immortality."

Analogues to wild-tame interactions form part of cultural history. Both our wild and taming tendencies need their due as ingredients of growth. The metaphor of making space for ourselves is important, space for creative interplay of tendencies. Tamer elements can act as a containing function for wild ones as balance shifts and the system as a whole grows and learns what is possible, surviving suffocation-shatter.

I'd like to bring in David Bohm (2002), a physicist. He and Matte-Blanco have a lot in common. David Bohm writes about implicate and explicate orders. The explicate order touches the multiplicity and diversity of creation, individuals, surfaces, separation, distinctions, space-time causality, all that we name this and that, akin to Matte-Blanco's asymmetrical consciousness. You are you, I am I, I am not you, you are not me – our perception of separateness.

The implicate order is analogous to Matte-Blanco's symmetrical unconscious tending towards ineffable invisibility, everything connected to everything else. In surface perception there are gaps of separation. In implicate depths everything resonates with, influences, and is influenced by everything or, at least, everything in a variable set. Matte-Blanco and Bohm overlap in recognizing two modes of being, perception, experiencing, concurrently working in various ways, both always going on. In the asymmetrical, explicate dimension I am not you, you are not I, while in the symmetrical, implicate order I am you, you are me, we are all each other in an ineffably permeable mode of being. There can be many kinds of relationships between these two orders of being. They can be opposed to each other in mutually antagonistic tensions or cooperative and co-nourishing or both. There are times antagonism leads to growth and lack of tension to stagnation, either can be creative and/ or destructive in myriad ways with many kinds of outcomes. One might posit conflict more likely for the asymmetrical-explicate mode and flow or continuum more characteristic of the symmetrical-implicate, but a capacity for reversal may straddle their interplay. The play of both add to plasticity, richness of experiencing as well as resourceful survival.

If you are going to have an operation, you want the surgeon to be well rooted in the asymmetrical-explicate order, able to differentiate between organs, their functions, locations and quirks. You want him to have the knowledge and skill to do a good job surgically. If you are seeing a therapist you need the latter to have a balance between asymmetry/explicate and symmetry/implicate, someone who can be empathic yet both identify and dis-identify, connect and detach with your felt being, linked and separate. The interplay of capacities evolve, bring us to different places, enable us to sense and think about things in many ways – a process that goes on all lifelong.

One moment we feel at one with everything. Another moment we feel detached, separate. We can feel at one with oneself or at odds with oneself, dissociated from oneself, these and more at the same time as well as sequentially. We can feel confused – how can we be at one and lost or detached at the same time? It is because of the way we are made up. We are made up of both tendencies and both are needed parts of our life.

In ordinary, everyday life we often feel both tendencies at work. We are not totally one or the other. We may even feel a certain frustration not being wholly one or the other, oscillating or caught in tensions between, hopefully, often enough, a cooperative tension. At other moments there is satisfaction, pleasure that one can feel them both, pleasures of separation, pleasures of connection, distinction-union.

One of the frustrating things about our nature is that we are not one thing or the other. We are always both and more. We cannot confine and reduce ourselves to one system, a fact that can be irritating and rewarding. Very often we do not know the source of our frustration. We blame something else, parents, society, or whatever your favorite blame objects. Not that parents, society, and other blame objects aren't trouble sources. They are. But the difficulty goes farther and is part of our inherent makeup. Inherent pain and difficulty, inherent pleasures, part of who we are, including part of how we make meaning and meaning makes us. We are called upon to make space for who we are, make room for learning about our makeup.

I would like to apply the distinction-union idea – a structure made of multiple systems – to the life experience of Rabbi Nachman, a descendent of the Baal Shem Tov. The Baal Shem Tov ("Master of the Good Name") was a Jewish mystic in Russia, founder of what came to be Chassidic communities, one who lives devotionally from the inside. He was something of a revolutionary in his time, respecting legal aspects of his Jewish heritage yet emphasizing emotional life, living close to God and humanity from the depths. The inner spirit of life gives life, lifts life. He felt at home in nature and spent time meditating and praying in woods. He inspired and supported followers to pay attention to deep feelings, not only mental analysis. In a sense, this opened channels to a more democratic relationship to God. A rough parallel might be ancient India where the populace listened to the priest's recitation, a gap between the uneducated masses and the elite few. This had parallels with ancient Judaism too, where the literate priests conducted services, read the Holy Scriptures, and conveyed God's desire. In theory, at least, Buddhism went beyond encased social structures, not confining enlightenment to any particular caste. Through the Baal Shem Tov as a significant channel Judaism embraced the heart as a pathway to closeness to God. Of course, the primacy of love was always built into Torah – love God with all you heart, soul, might. But with the Baal Shem Tov in his time, the life and law of the heart opened new channels of living and worship for more people regardless of social class. A universalism of access to the Divine was gaining ground in links to spiritual life.

Not that literate learning is unimportant. It can inform discernment of feeling and at times shed clarity in complex situations. But now it is commonplace to ask what does your heart tell you and what is God telling you in your heart. The part in you akin to illiterate Rabbi Akiva in back of the shul as a child reciting the aleph-bet with all his heart, a devotional path to God, more, nearness to God expressed in ways one can.

Rabbi Nachman was a great grandson of the Baal Shem Tov who advocated talking with God, telling Him everything, something like an ordinary conversation, although charged with the depth of awareness of divine communion. Since God is everywhere all the time access is everywhere all the time, you have but to open your heart and feel the connection, a very special contact in which a lot can happen in a short time.

Rabbi Nachman's experiences portray rich variations of distinction-union extremes. He was no stranger to different size emotions. Rabbi Schneur Zalman whose *Tanya* (1779, 2020) laid the foundation for the Chabad branch of Judaism, wrote of different capacities as vehicles through which to commune with the Divine, e.g., thinking, feeling, sensing, action as preferred modes of contact. For Rabbi Nachman emotion was a treasured vehicle, often harder to ride than a wild horse or perhaps mad winds or waves would be better metaphors. One moment he felt very close to God, another extremely far away and hopeless about ever being close again (Eigen, 2012, Part 2). Near-far, such a basic dimension in experience, like towards-away, up-down, in-out. Too near, too far, not near enough, not far enough, part of the palette of emotional life.

One of the jobs in therapy is to help support growth of tolerance of interplay of capacities, if not accept at least begin to tolerate what different tendencies have to contribute. For example, near-far opens worlds of emotional riches if we can mine them. When I talked about parts of the self with Bion he said something like, "There really aren't 'parts' of the self. I know we speak that way. But there is just *you*." Yes, just *me* undergoing all kinds of dramas and unknown nuances, depths. I'm glad there wasn't the term "bipolar" to depict Nachman's extremes of experience in his day. He just underwent them, dealt with the flood of states life brought him. Moments so far from God he felt he would never be close again, moments so close to God he felt he would never be far. I hear Bion saying – this is just you – all of this – you. Maybe a little like Whitman saying, "I am multitudes." Winnicott, too, valued extremes of experience, even prayed, "Lord, may I be alive when I die." After all, how many times can you experience the moment of your death – what a loss to miss it!

What Nachman experienced was not mere mania or depression. He experienced ecstatic closeness and agonized loss: heaven and the pit, the abyss. I don't think he would have wanted to miss what is possible to experience in relation to God and the terror and wonder of being, so filled with spirit, so empty.

At one moment he might wake up and say, "No one has ever lived a day like this!" At another, he might say, "No one has ever died a death like this!" Absolutizing moments brings out everything they have to offer yet they are situated in a larger frame of reference. He called his emotions messengers. They brought messages from God. Messengers sent to find someone who needs them and Nachman received them as gifts. There are so many stories in which messengers never found their recipient and others in which they did. There is a Talmudic saying that every uninterpreted dream is an unopened letter from God – dreams as messengers even if many are indecipherable. That is one of the amazing things about our experience, hidden dimensions in themselves. So much of what happens deep within is unknown and indecipherable yet sometimes dimly sensed, a dim sense that opens being. A Mystery keeps giving us itself without our ever being able to decipher it, one moment a void, another fullness without measure.

A dynamic that combines the simply human with the mystical in the psalms, moments of union and loss, empty-full, presence-absence. "I go to bed weeping and wake up laughing" (Psalm 27). My mood or state depending, in part, how near-far I feel from God, so many cries of pain and joy in the psalms. "Where are you, Lord?" "Why are you hiding you face from me?" "I cry to you from the abyss." And when God shows His face, shines His Light, the psalmist lights up, joyfully singing and dancing. The psalms are filled with emotional extremes, like Rabbi Nachman. God is close, I'm happy; God is far, I'm in despair. I think of Melanie Klein describing an infant's feelings in terms of the mother's presence-absence or quality of being. Or Freud's fort-da, the back and forth of a maternal link. What does closeness feel like? What does far feel like? So close, so far. Jesus about to join the Eternal Power, "Father why have you deserted me?" Or Job's wondrous cry and amazing affirmation, "Yay though You slay me, yet will I trust You." The same tension, dual structure, distinction-union everywhere.

Find you favorite psalms and trace the emotional movements. Now, although these emotional extremes were parts of Nachman's life, he did not wish them away. He wished to open them, follow their pathways, let them open him, open his heart. His broken heart – he would say speak to God from your broken heart. We feel through Rabbi Nachman a broken heart speaking and in this we feel healing as well. Speak to God from your pain, say everything. Is this Freud? "Tell me everything." It's hard to read about Rabbi Nachman without thinking of free association, letting wounds speak along with strengths. Rabbi Nachman turned his broken heart into a method of healing, a way of speaking with God. Rather than obliterate or escape from it he turned it into a method of approach, a seeking. In the words of Rabbi Menachem Mendel of Kotzk, fifteen years Nachman's junior (I have not read that they ever met), "Nothing is more whole than a broken heart." Two resonant souls, in this regard united in spirit.

QUESTION I: I thought up to this point that the goal in clinical practice was to overcome splitting and separation and become unified. However, you talked about distinction and union as both important and necessary. This makes me feel relieved, but at the same time bewildered. Distinction and union. How do I achieve balance between these two?

RESPONSE I: Well, that's between you and God. How do you achieve balance? I don't have balance. I'm off balanced, imbalanced. Balance is just a word, an inclusive word. It means not rejecting either side. Inside has a biography, a development to undergo. You have to develop this inside, enrich it so that it can enrich you. It needs to be nourished and needs to nourish you. In knowing about balance do you know what happens when you are imbalanced? I think of one foot Torah, a bit like one finger Zen or the sound of one hand clapping. A man asks Rabbi Hillel to explain the whole Torah while the man stands on one foot (which is better than not having a leg to stand on). "What is hateful to you, do not do to your neighbor," Hillel responds. "That is the whole of it, the rest explanation. Now go study."

If I am on one foot I feel shaky, leaning to keep my balance, almost falling over, perhaps falling over. I can hop on one foot but not very long. Well, sometimes you only have one foot and that actually may be a longer time than you realize, maybe a good part of a lifetime and you have to learn to live with imbalance. Maybe there's even such a thing as creative imbalance. Hillel was a gentle man, his teachings kindly rather than severe, taking the edge off one's severity to oneself yet a motivating, even inspiring kindliness, prompting further search and a better balance of tendencies.

Here is a story from my one meeting with Winnicott in 1968. At some point he went to sit on his couch and tightly screwed up his body on the edge of it trying to figure out how to communicate something he was in touch with – how to touch me with what touched him. He told me a story about a woman he was working with. She was trying to center his face in her handheld mirror as he sat behind her. He could see his image in the mirror was off-center and moved his head so that it would be centered. The instant he did that he realized it was a mistake. The next session the woman told him, "If you had done that six months ago I'd be back in the hospital." Sometimes trying to help can be harmful. One of the points of the story is that it is important that you grow to the point where you can tolerate being off-centered.

This woman's mother needed to be the center of her child's existence. The mother could not bear not being the center. The psychoanalyst had to bear not being the center, bear being off-balanced. In this case a kind of therapeutic off-balance or what I like to sometimes call creative off-balance.

There can be mixtures of balance and off-balance in the distinction-union structure that function variable ways. Building tolerance for each side, each sub-system may be crucial one moment, but tolerating lack of symmetry, their imbalance can also be crucial. We speak of being centered but there is also value in building tolerance for being off-center or decentered as well. No one is "centered" or psychically "balanced" all the time – that is an idealization. We have a lot of messy mixtures to work and be with moment to moment throughout an hour or day or lifetime. No one has a perfect homeostasis. You have to be dead to approximate that. Life has both peace and turbulence, and all sorts of mixes and possibilities. T.S. Eliot calls April the cruelest month because life springs anew through the earth's cold crust. So, if I have any advice maybe it's respect your not knowing how to integrate these tendencies because no one knows. It's a matter of trial and error and seeing what works in your own life as you keep growing. No one can do that but you but there may be more helpers deep within than you know.

QUESTION 2: You talked about the psyche not being able to withstand its own intensity and breaking or exploding in the process. In Buddhism, in order to realize the truth you have to let things go, let go of worldly things. Is there a connection between what you are saying and Buddhism?

RESPONSE 2: I don't know, but there are different moments, often very different moments, states, dimensions, paths. In one moment there may be more flow, letting go, emptying out. In another you might experience shatter, a psychic explosion. In certain instances, particularly psychosis but not only this, Bion pictures the psyche exploding, a kind of big bang, bits and pieces of thought, sensation, and emotion scattered through space flying faster and faster away from each other and the point of origin. Points of peace and turbulence all parts of what we can experience (and experiencing ourselves experiencing). Different capacities, different states. I can adopt an attitude of not holding on to anything, emptying out, just be with whatever comes. I can also investigate what comes and try to get ideas what it is made of. Another possibility is building more tolerance for intensity, flow, blockage. In his way, Rabbi Nachman teaches there is no contradiction between emptiness-fullness. With nearness he feels fuller, with distance emptier, both can play positive roles in the course of growth. When you ask a question I try not to hold on to anything, just be, empty, see what comes. Maybe I'll have a helpful response, maybe not. There is a value in just being present with the question. But on other planes capacities in me are interacting with the question. As I've noted, there's no contradiction between different states of being. They are all asking for development, all part of the richness of who we are or what we can be.

Different religions, different groups emphasize different states. They become specialists cultivating particular paths, moments, possibilities. All play a role in cultural life past and present. So many flowers, plants, critters to appreciate, be with, learn from. In certain ways, there is cultural division of labor, each adding gifts of perception, know-how, and practice. Not everyone can do everything well. Part of our learning is lifelong discovery of what we *can* do and be, our special contribution to the amazing sum of life. Different people work with different areas of experience and we gain by sharing. The French explored certain avenues of cooking, the Korean another. That applies to psychic exploration as well. We are all explorers of different states, how life tastes to us. There are so many ways, as there are so many poets. Exploration doesn't stop. As long as I keep breathing I keep exploring Eigen-life, whatever that is. Me. You are your specialist, a specialist of how life tastes to you. It's not a matter of one or the other. You report to us what you find in the path of letting go and emptiness and Nachman reports what he found through the path of the broken heart. Both are parts of our being, valuable parts of experience. In *The Sensitive Self* (2007) I talked about psychic taste buds, different ways of tasting life, and all the ways we are called to give expression to the taste of love. Only you can do your breathing, your tasting, but we have a lot to offer each other as well as ourselves.

QUESTION 3: When you talked about symmetrical tendencies I found it very similar to Jung's idea of collective unconscious. Can you explain a little bit about how these two might be different?

RESPONSE 3: The collective unconscious is a very big topic. Many archetypes, constellations, structures developed through evolution and ways we do not know. That already may be a difference from the symmetrical unconscious which becomes less structured the deeper it goes.

At the moment, I'm thinking of Jung positing a crossing the bridge archetype associated with fear of bridge crossing. Will it hold me? Is it strong enough, made well enough? In very ancient times bridges may have been less well built than today and the danger of falling greater. There is a background of experience involved in this fear, and while it is part of the collective unconscious it has links with the personal unconscious as well, e.g., the song rock-a-bye baby and the danger of baby falling, cradle, and all. An archetype with roots in the personal, the personal with roots in the archetype. Falling is a danger all lifelong, whether a plane crash, loss of balance as a child or elder, and much else. We even call the loss of an imaginary paradise a fall.

Cross of water imagery is part of many mythic narratives. In the Bible, Abraham crosses the water to begin a new life. Buddha speaks of going to the other side, crossing the water to Nirvana. Water, too, is part of birth and nourishment that sustains life. I used to hear teachers say we are mostly made up of water, although it did not feel that way when I fell down and bled. Through baptism with water we are reborn. Life imagery spans many dimensions, at once structural and historical. Birth is a bio-psycho-spiritual image that runs through our lives from beginning to end.

One of Jung's emphases is the importance of individuation and growth towards wholeness, in part making use of and individuating from the collective unconscious. Organizational patterns are part of both collective and personal. There may be symmetrical elements operating as well, with archetypes perhaps operating something like Matte-Blanco's sets. But it appears that differentiated patterns Jung emphasizes would, in Matte-Blanco's system, be more a part of a kind of asymmetrical consciousness, although both would be at work. I wish I could do better and perhaps in time we will. You might read Henry Elkin's papers (1956, 1972) for his discussion of collective-communal in relation to Jung and Buber. It might add a little to the picture.

If there are no more questions at the moment, I'd like to move towards closing, continuing to use Nachman as a meditative base. You might say we have two paths so far in Nachman, emotions as messengers and speaking from the broken heart, which has a lot in common with free association in psychoanalysis, speaking your pain from your pain. Linked with these were dialectics of closeness-distance, being too close, too far, and the dynamics of emptiness-fullness associated with them, our ongoing challenge of finding ways that work.

A third path for Nachman has to do with song and dance and the joyous clapping of hands. To me it seems as if in some ways he felt life as musical, a musical universe. He felt the whole universe singing, blades of grass are singing. If you are a shepherd, you will want to sing with the blades of grass or play an instrument with them. Music helps the grass grow so sheep will have a more nutritious meal. Everything is alive and singing. One is close to God through singing and dancing. However, Nachman had a very special dance: his dance was so still you could not see him move. A deep, motionless dance was a way of praying. In another state of prayer you had to clap your hands. So you have the broken heart and the joyous dance, prayers of tears and prayers of singing and clapping. The clapping hands universe reminds me of the Buddhist sound of one hand clapping. In Zen Buddhism, too, there are mountains that live, mountains that dance and in the psalms mountains live, dance, sing, rejoice. And so we have Nachman's third path: the music of the universe in song and dance and bodily expression. You have to live your way into it. You have to imagine stillness so profound that stillness is dancing. When I say his dance was so still you couldn't see his body move, he is talking about stillness dancing.

There were moments when Nachman sang and danced with such high-pitched jubilation he would say, "Ah! No one has ever sung a song like this! No one has ever danced a dance like this!" There is a lot of singing and dancing in the Bible. So much dancing by women, King David with Torah and women, psalms filled with longing, sadness, triumph, worry and the last Psalm 150: "Let's all bang the cymbals, play the drums, blow the horns, dance and joy." Joy of existence, joy of spirit, joy of God – an ancient path humans know well.

I feel all the states are connected, something touched by Matte-Blanco's symmetrical unconscious and Bion's sense of foundational infinity. Broken heart, joyous dance, joyous song, sorrowful song, the universe singing, stillness singing, one in the many, many in the one, a name of God that means one, a name of God that means many, moments of distinction-union structures.

We have spoken about emotions as messengers, speaking from a broken heart, joyous singing, dancing, and clapping. Nachman's fourth path is constant struggle. Nachman bemoaned that while others have found their niche, calling, place, he never found his. He was always recreating himself every minute. Every hour was new. He was being created by every moment, by every hour. No resting place. Constant struggle with his old self, habits, ways because the new kept pushing him farther. Bion, too, shared sensitivity to the newness of every moment in his own way. For example, he said if you think you are seeing the same patient you are seeing the wrong patient. Heraclitus's river covers time in general: you can never see the same patient twice, emphasizing newness of experience and life.

In some way Nachman saw himself as a lifelong patient, both God and he were patients of each other. There would always be struggle between old and new self, birth struggle ever emerging. We are born all lifelong. Nachman felt he had no resting place in the unceasing struggle between old and new. Life doesn't rest; psyche never stops.

It took time before Nachman was able to declare the constant struggle he hid for so long. He said if the soul comes out into the public too fast it can get damaged. It needs to germinate, baking time. It needs time away from public fights and arguments, it needs to be nursed, hidden, private, lay low. Then comes a time when it must go public. There is a time when the self grows through hiding and a time when it grows through struggle. Again dual parts of a structure with the same roots, one in many, many in one – a self with many parts and tendencies needing to hide and nurse, needing publication and struggle. Hiding-and-struggling, part of emotional, attitudinal dialectics.

Nachman's fifth path has to do with knowing and not knowing. Sometimes he felt like he knew such high spiritual levels that he was afraid to say what he saw. If he showed what he knew everyone would pass out. In related fashion, he ordered a companion to burn certain of his writings when he died, writings he felt humanity would not know what to do with. Humanity was not ready for such strong revelations, such profound oneness with faith. Along with a sense that no one ever felt or knew like this before he could also feel that no one ever preached like this before. Still, he went farther saying, "Yes, yes but even better is my not knowing. My not-knowing is even higher than my knowing."

In common with Buddha he tailored messages to the hearer. With the unlearned he supported what they could know. With the learned he would bring out what was missing, so much more to go. With one individual he would support knowing, with another question attachment to knowing and get back to unknowing. With one individual, the little he knew was abundant, with another the more he knew stood in the way. Again paradoxical dialectic of knowing-unknowing, branches from a deep root.

In our last minutes today I'd like to try a little meditation. Let me give a tiny bit of background. The Baal Shem Tov used to go into the woods and pray from his heart and being. Later generations would say, "Well, we don't know the prayers but we can still find the place." Still later generations would say, "We don't know the prayers or place, but we can go into the woods." And even later generations were not even sure where the woods were. With each generation more disappeared and got lost.

Now let us do something in reverse, a vision of finding along with losing. Let us all go into the forest. Picture going into the forest even though you don't know where it is and you don't know where you are going. Maybe you and I can shut our eyes and picture going into the forest. You don't have to know where the place is but you find it, you don't know how. Your legs, your steps led to it, a feeling somewhere in your chest perhaps, some mysterious sense hard to pin down. You find the place and now you try to remember the prayer. The prayer that goes with the place. You're afraid you won't be able to remember it, can't remember it. Listen deeply. What prayer comes to you, almost comes to you? Feel the prayer. If you can't find it make one up and feel the prayer that wants to be born in you, that wants to give you birth. Your prayer. Let it come from anywhere at all. Have no presuppositions about this prayer. Let it form in you. Let it form you.

After finding the prayer, let it go. Remember only the feeling of the prayer. Stay with the prayer feeling. If you were to die now, is that a feeling that you can die with? If not, move it around, change it. Find a feeling you can die with. Feel that feeling. Let that feeling be your center. Let it touch you. Touch it. That feeling is your life.

[After some time hearing the breathing, the silence...]

See you in the morning.

Chapter 3

Day 3

Morning: miracles of everyday

I see that the survivors are here. People who survived the first two days and managing the third. That means you probably are the ones who really want to be here or forced to come for reasons I don't know about.

When we were talking about an internal catastrophic explosion someone said she doesn't feel the explosiveness, she feels frozen. I was speaking about a psychic catastrophe described by Bion (1970, Chapter 2) that goes along with a whole series of possible changes. He depicted a psychic Big Bang on the one hand and zeroing out on the other hand, maximum-minimum emotions that are counterparts. There is a whole spectrum of in-between states. There is a type of negativism that can blot out shock, I can't, I won't, an evacuating refusal, a kind of sibling of denial. There is a kind of rageful no that blots out the full catastrophe, dulling a primal explosion with a counter-explosion. There are different qualities of frozenness, e.g., being frozen in a state of shock or fear or self-protective hiding, trying to find a safe place. There can be varying states of numbness, "numbing out," detachment, loss of feeling, loss of self-feeling, gradual or rapid disappearance of self, different qualities of not being there. It may seem as if there are switches that turn emotional lights on and off. Our capacity to feel can take many turns depending on inner-outer conditions.

Yesterday someone commented on the meaning of Malkut, the tenth Sephira. She learned that Malkut meant kingdom, associated with being empowered, very different from my emphasis on its association with shatter, torn, and broken. Each thread has its place. There is enormous play of power, military, and despotic as well as creative on planet earth. There is the work of love and a destructive force within and without. Malkut is a domain of time, space, action, body, and all human capacities. It is profoundly paradoxical that brokenness contends with a wish to be whole, challenge without end. Is it possible to have a sense of brokenness and wholeness at the same time? It is one of the central paradoxes of human experience.

To be broken and empowered – it's not a matter of one or the other. One of the great empowerments we have is the work of healing, to help make broken aspects of life, self, world a little better, to the extent we can. It is a lifelong learning experience, always more to go, with interferences within and without. Yet it is work in which dimensions keep opening, life keeps opening. We have many capacities with many powers, and learning to partner them and them us is still embryonic.

I see Joon Ho passed out a diagram of the Sephirot. If you study it or just stare at it meditatively like a mandala, you will see different parts interacting, entering different relations with each other. If you use the metaphor of energy, there is flow in all directions, now more-less, different capacities dominant-recessive, combining-retreating in varied ways.

People have been making typologies of capacities, temperaments, and personalities for a long time. In ancient Greece, four humors or temperaments. In 19th century thirty drives. Years ago in school we learned about 20th-century factor psychology. Many maps of elusive territory – try drawing your own or living without one.

This morning I'd like to speak about parts of a play I wrote, "Something Wrong," from *Flames From the Unconscious: Trauma, Madness and Faith* (2009). There are several versions, one with Grace and Dr. Z, one with Grace alone (also published in *Moondance*, 2006). In another, Merle Molofsky divided Grace into three Graces played by herself, Elizabeth Singer, and Amanda George. This version was enacted at the National Psychological Association for Psychoanalysis, the International Forum for Psychoanalytic Education, and The New School. A Swedish version was performed by Karen Swenson in Sweden at varied mental health venues followed by discussion.

The name Dr. Z is based on Winnicott's depictions of X, Y, and Z dimensions representing the time a baby is separated from its mother. X time, mother comes back, baby is OK. X + Y time, mother comes back, there is more difficulty but things work out. X + Y + Z time and there is ineradicable damage in the baby. The baby is not the same. In the Z dimension there is a lasting alteration of the personality.

Most of the time life goes on after this deformation. Sometimes a baby will die from lack of contact but most go on living after they undergo this change. If they are lucky, some of them will become your patients.

For the current printed chapter that you are reading in this book, I will not be quoting the play verbatim as I did in Seoul. Aspects are paraphrased, added to, commented on here. You can find the play itself in *Flames from the Unconscious* (2009) and *Moondance* (2006).

The play is about a woman, Grace, who was repeatedly hospitalized and medicated. Through psychoanalytic psychotherapy over many years she became hospital and mediation free, living at the edge of her own experience – I am tempted to add living at the creative edge of her personality.

There is no one outcome or journey for people who have been hospitalized with psychological problems. Bion liked to speak of breakdown, breakup, breakthrough. Outcomes are variable, some better or worse than others. As a child, I often heard that no two snowflakes are the same. Perhaps I intuited what was meant then but it took some time to consciously realize that this saying was about more than snowflakes, it is about us. Grace is one particular character and this afternoon we will speak of another. Warning: handle psychological perceptions with care. There is no one journey or goal and what is said of one individual may or may not apply to another or even the same person at another time.

The title of the play, "Something Wrong," associates with themes we have mentioned, linking with brokenness, shatter, personality undergoing catastrophic processes. Sometimes people ask, "Why did you choose the name Grace? Why Grace?" It means just what you think – grace. The possibility of grace in shatter, including resonance with the holy and whole. I am thinking of a custom to save broken pieces of a handmade clay pot and put them together as best one can, then paint over them with a transparent gold binding and one experiences the broken pieces and whole together.

Grace begins by speaking of feeling wrong and more, a sense of being wrong, *the* wrong. A sense of something off in personality, with one's being, almost as far back as she can remember. As a little girl she searched for someone who did not see her as The Wrong, someone for whom she mattered. She almost found it in teachers, but not quite.

Her hospitalizations started in her teens. She wondered if something good would happen in the hospital that would correct the wrong but the wrong seemed to spread. Those around her seemed to have the wrong too, even those who tried to help her. The Wrong was swallowing up the world.

We begin with a sense of something wrong, even a feeling that I am the Wrong. The Wrong stains being, my being. Does it disguise me? Is it me? A basic state that takes many forms. Not only psychosis in a hospital but a psychotic dimension of life. We joke about people being quite mad as a whole, life as mad and maddening, something rotten in the state of Denmark, in the world, perhaps part of human feelings since the beginning of time.

Grace likens this feeling of something wrong to abuse. Someone sticks the wrong into her and for a time it comes in waves, surges like sexual feeling. It ebbs and comes again like a traumatic memory, a traumatic happening right now.

One way of picturing this is to say parents have a bad feeling inside them and when it builds to a point where they can't take it, they put it into the child. They use the child as a toilet or container or garbage dump for their bad feelings. It can come out in different ways: yelling at the child or silently transmitting it via psychic osmosis, a feeling in the air, a feeling in the skin, seeing the child with a bad eye.

A colleague tells a story about a patient's father seeing her as a child demon or wild woman, not human, an inhuman child menace. The child builds up her personality to fight against feeling an inhuman menace. But now she is fighting against something inside her. He has put this picture inside her and she is using what strength she has to fight against it.

Our bad feeling can mount up if we don't deal with it. We put it inside other people. We can make other people feel horrible to relieve ourselves, like going to the bathroom, using others as toilets for bad feelings. Hopefully, when someone comes into therapy and begins to do this, the therapy situation can help modulate these feelings over time, creating a deep feedback loop so that exchange of feelings becomes less destructive. This is not something a baby or child can do well enough by itself when bad things are being put inside them.

There was a point when Grace saw a knife in another's face, a knife inside that lives in blood and pain, a famished knife, a hungry knife. Is this psychotic hallucination-delusion or perception of an emotional reality, emotional truth? Perhaps it depends how one relates to such perceptions, how one *can* relate to them.

Grace recounted moments as a little girl when she turned to Jesus, someone who knew the Wrong, pain, and death and triumphed over it. Jesus as a lightning rod for the Wrong of this world. It took time but she began to appreciate the whole sequence of agony, dying to oneself and rebirth, coming alive in new ways, a basic pattern of experience I've come to call a rhythm of faith (Eigen, 2004).

For moments she could experience the more of life, then fall back into the Wrong. She had hoped Jesus would clean the Wrong away but she feared it was part of her essence, part of her pulse – not the whole, but a dreadful part.

Very often turning to religion can help someone feel better for a time. This kept happening for Grace but then she comes back to herself and the bad feeling comes back, states she is left to deal with alone. As though God helps for moments then lets the person drop down to life on earth again with a bad feeling still there yet some relief that it can go away for a while. There are even moments of joy which transcend the Wrong or eclipse it, moments one appreciates, but too often the Wrong comes back with a wallop. One moment: I am a trauma I will never recover from. Another moment: I am trauma that passes through death to life. Perhaps at times a better term than death is Winnicott's (1974) "primitive agonies."

Grace speaks of a line from a psalm that expresses something basic for her: *"I am poor and destitute, my heart has died within me."* Such a human paradox that a confession of death makes her feel alive. To have a state recognized, validated, words that say what she feels, the relief of truth. My heart has died within me. Someone knows. A lasting grace of the psalms is their confession of emotional truths. What I'm feeling exists, the psalmist knows about it. Acknowledgment of death enables her to feel a moment of aliveness. Pretense that this death is not there makes her feel even deader. All I have to do in such a moment is reflect back the truth of feeling. Patient: "My heart has died within me." Therapist: "Yes, your heart has died within you and I feel it."

Grace wonders if there ever was a time before Something Wrong and thinks not, fears not. There was something wrong, even in the Garden of Eden: a snake telling lies, a tempter with links to destruction. Given the pain of her life, the pain of existence, Grace says, amazingly, "I am ashamed of not hating God more." A remark I take as a tribute to intimate relationship.

If you are in a close relationship with God, even a doubt-full relationship, you are emboldened, propelled, invited to speak your heart out, as Rabbi Nachman encourages, speak your broken heart. What is breaking you? How to say it? "I hate you, God, for what you do to me." When my brother died, run over by a truck, till the end of her days in her late eighties, my mother felt He had something to answer for. In a way, she could not wait to confront Him and take Him to account. Was God her child too? It is part of intimacy to confront and challenge. If a woman like Grace feels ashamed for not hating God more, such shame/hate is part of a faith-link. Can God take what he puts into us? Can God take what he puts into our heart? We confront God with what he puts into us.

Grace has a realization that we are the garden, the liar and the lies, storytelling snakes. We are the sea, the air, the animals, the flowers. We are destructive creativity, as God is. Creative dysregulation.

Some people really lie and pass real lies off as truth. Garden of Eden, Garden of Evil. We as a group make up some whoppers, like making up a God story and saying it really happened when it is really a literary event, a spiritual event. We tell stories about a destructive urge in the Garden of Life. Are we afraid to say that we like this destructive urge? That this urge is a way into life? That our stories are all too often emotional truth in disguise or, better, truth wide open? We need our stories to keep in contact with ourselves, to let life speak.

We have families of tendencies inside, outside, between. One that I remember well as a child, destroying can be a pleasure. Building blocks, knocking them down. Destructive creation. I liked ripping things up, breaking up a tower of blocks. I don't like getting hurt by your destruction. There were moments as a child I liked to hurt people. I liked hurting my mother sometimes. I liked seeing her distress and worry if it was not too much. I liked to build. I liked to destroy. I liked to cause pain. I liked to ruin things. There were times I felt more alive when I was bad. There was a devil in me that liked to make a mess of things and hear mama say, "You're a little devil." Well, that's cute, but what about someday being a big one? I don't feel as good when I'm a goody-goody. Grace is honest about it. Therapy opens the door.

Grace is baffled by her own religious devotion, her sincerity, and her thought that the garden is destructive birthing, the garden nourishes destruction. Are there snakes inside the caring mother and nursing infant? Are religions mad to imagine destructive free life while they destroy? Do we imagine being expelled from the Garden because we need to preserve a fantasy place that is destruction-free, a place to look back at or forward to, a destruction-free place within?

The garden tells us it is good to be alive yet destruction comes with aliveness. Scientists tell us our universe began with a destructive act, an explosion that led to us and all we know and see and participate in. We are appalled at the need to destroy and try to think of ways to outwit destruction; use destruction to someday return to, find, or create a destruction-free place, a destruction-free existence. A place we can only imagine. Are there ways imagining makes it so? What is real? Making believe destruction does not exist? Hiding? Doing what we can?

Remember, we are dealing with a psychotic self or part of the self in individuals being destroyed by psychosis. Being destroyed by one's own destructiveness. I once had a patient (you can meet her in Chapter 6 of *The Sensitive Self*, 2004) who spoke of a shredder inside, a shredder that seemed to have a penchant, urge, and ability to shred potentially good thoughts in her mind. Destruction everywhere. She fights to stay alive, seeking relatively destruction-free moments, knowing that she is fighting against time, buying time against the fact that there never was a place without destruction, that it's a part of her, a part of life.

For years Grace was making believe destruction did not exist. For years her parents emotionally abused her. One can whitewash and blackwash experience, either way making believe it is not there. Making believe you are not there can spiral into something awful, although it may work awhile. Better the realization it is there: I don't know what to do with it but it is there. I'm not always going to look the other way.

What about all the myths in which you die or turn into stone or something awful happens if you actually see the thing itself. What about this sensation, perception, thought that one's essence is the bad in itself, not good in itself. By now you must be discovering that Grace is a very bright, philosophical, artistic woman in her own way, an artist in finding the bad in herself. An artist in finding ways to stay alive against great odds and sometimes alive in wondrous ways.

Some of you must have worked with people whose self-hate is a key or a kernel. Grace has moments where self-hate is mirrored back to her in the news. She tells a story on TV about a girl killed by her step-father and her mother in jail for child abuse, weeping, insisting she was a good mother. A picture emerged of the girl tied to a chair, eating dog food, beaten, starved, thin as a feather. I think of Wilhelm Fliess's son, Robert Fliess (1973) writing about particular dynamics of the abuser feeling right to punish and discipline the child in an attempt to rid the child of Satan (in Grace's case, The Wrong), a dynamic that seems part of a larger social psychosis. One rationalizes (deludes) oneself into thinking one is helping the child, educating, exorcising the bad. I remember a phrase from years ago, "beating the devil out of her." In trying to kill the bad thing the bad thing kills them, marred by their own aggression.

In contrast to the murdered child, Grace felt lucky. She is still alive, talking about the wrong with me, two people who can practice being wrong together and see what happens, exchanging words, feelings, thoughts. Human beings who care are lucky to have each other, lucky to leave each other, and return to be together again, protected by limits of time. Each day the news adds another story that vanishes. Yet we have the chance to build together, partnering our psyches together. Grace would not let herself feel she was the girl who died, that would be an injustice to the girl's real death. But she acknowledged the emotional truth that the girl tied up in the chair and murdered was in her, part of her.

"Let us tolerate being wrong together." Not a bad prescription as a part of human relations.

Unlike Grace, the murdered child could not get up and leave. She could not freely come and go. In a way, the time limits and structure of therapy made our being together safer. She could walk out the door any time she wants and return, if she wants, for her next session. Therapy was not exactly like being incarcerated and if it felt that way she could tell me if she wants to if her insides let her. To what extent did the child have to pretend that what was happening to her wasn't happening? To what extent did she have to make believe she was not being abused? To what extent did moments of honest self-assertion run the risk of stimulating more parental aggression?

Grace wondered if the girl tried to put up a fight and the stepfather killed her. She felt she gave in to her shameful feelings and did not act them out and went crazy instead of being killed. And in this bit of self-estimation you could hear a taint of self-denigration. To what extent is going crazy a kind of self-protection in the service of survival? Both families, the murdered girl's and her own, lacked resources to work with aggressive tendencies which oscillated between spiraling and zeroing out. A fuller landscape of emotional colors lacked conditions for growth. Through hospitalizations Grace found her way into therapy she could use in the service of building resources for more therapy, resources to learn to work better with what is troubling and allow a wider range of positive experience to develop.

Many of Grace's concerns sounded basic themes of the human conditions. How can we survive each other and with what quality? In what ways can we make room for the wrong that never goes away? Can we work with it to benefit life? William Blake calls Satan Energy and Energy Eternal Delight. We have been trying to work with the negative for eons. Freud felt that frustration of wishes was an inevitable part of life and emphasized creative use of our energy as a way of working with conflicting tendencies and putting them to better use. Andre Green (1999) stressed learning to work with the negative in fresh ways. At one point Grace said, "I go into your Wrong, you go into mine. I find mine through yours, you through mine. To touch the worse. Most people try to get out of when the job is to get *into* it." A learning and reciprocity much desired, ever in need of practice and adjustment. I've often thought of the saying, "You can't step into the same river twice." My feeling has been more along the line to take the chance, find the resources, begin the learning of daring to step into it once, and once again.

A wonderful saying of Grace's: "Freedom is working with the Wrong." Partly a freedom from trying to make believe the wrong isn't there or is everything or more than it is. Also the freedom from having to be "right." Having to be right is such pressure, a burden, just as feeling essentially wrong is paralyzing.

As an adult, Grace makes the discovery that the emotional violence she felt as a child is acted out in the world everywhere – economic and military violence were really happening, not just in her family but all through society. Childhood nightmares were actually being lived in the world as a whole. Feared violence in childhood was more accurate with regard to human existence than she could have realized.

When Grace went to a restaurant and food she ordered did not arrive in a timely way, she was able to handle it much better than a patient Bion wrote about. When Bion's patient's waitress made a mistake he was so exasperated that his meal was ruined – spoiled. Something he hoped would be good went wrong. He could not recover or in his words, "That finished it!" (Bion, 1994, p. 79; see Day 1 of the present work). In contrast, Grace also felt catastrophic underpinnings but tried to figure out what was happening and situate it more realistically. Something was wrong but she did not want to go down all the way. She tried to figure a way out of the situation, a way to handle it. She wanted to try to keep her good feeling yet let the restaurant know that something was wrong. What happened to the food on one level felt catastrophic, the end of the world but on another it was just a time-space work problem. She went back and forth. She was generally happy in the restaurant and did not want to ruin the whole evening. A grown up part of her reached the point of being able to ask the waitress, "Where's the food?" or "How's the food coming?" without spoiling a good time. There was a time when saying anything would have been too much but now asking for the food was just asking for the food, to extent that was possible.

It was part of the background of her being that she was so used to making believe everything is OK, that saying the truth in a restaurant can become an existential crises, tension between something not being OK and catastrophic dread attached to emotional truth since childhood. On the other hand, she sometimes had emotional outbursts that turned her parents off and made things worse. I sometimes imagined she was at those moments like a baby screaming for help with pain or other distress and the parent put off rather than solicitous and helpful. Caught between concealment and outburst – her struggle to find a viable path in the restaurant was a maturational movement.

At another point Grace spoke of having a vision of human pain through the ages which made her weep. The perennial grief of humankind. I thought of a number of people I worked with who shared this experience in their own ways. A kind of cosmic weeping for the suffering of humanity mixed with loss and longing and care. I remember a hospitalized patient weeping like this recovering from an electroshock treatment. One easily can associate his empathic moment with voltage he experienced, but it felt like something more, perhaps an awakening to cosmic grief and need, as if the shock brought him closer to all pain of all people. Like Grace, they felt in contact with deep truth, deep life. Moments of being overtaken by a tragic dimension in human life. It would be wonderful if a psychiatrist can mirror the patient's feeling when the latter says, "I cry for all the pain in life." And the psychiatrist says, "I feel that way too."

You might say she was seeing pain everywhere like someone else might see fear everywhere or anger everywhere, expressing in a displaced way the pain she felt as a child that did not have anywhere to go.

At the moment I'm thinking of a man who told me about something that happened in a past therapy. He had several hospitalizations and after his last one bought a good quality FM radio with a wonderful sound. The music he played was so beautiful that he would start crying. When he shared his FM happiness and tears of beauty with his therapist she was baffled. She did not understand his need or why he would weep. She wanted to analyze the long-standing longing behind it. In a way, she was not wrong to touch his lifelong longing. On the other hand, she seemed to miss the beauty of music and tears.

Some years later he spoke of his deprived life and the tearful burst of beauty that filled him. In one session he found himself saying the music was giving birth to his heart. Not that he was heartless but this was a new heart dimension, born through beauty. It seemed to me that beauty might bring many people to tears, it did me. In a recent seminar I found myself saying beautiful music often has a tinge of sorrow in it.

There was a point where Grace felt relief from her tears and a point where they scared her. She feared she could go so far inside her tears that the outside world would be unreal. Or worse, that she could not get to it. As if she would have to choose between making contact with inside or outside reality. The challenge of being with both was seeking her. She had come a long way. Now even if outside felt unreal she could still perceive and think about it as if real. This was an important gain, to realize both inner-outer needed her attention. Working with inner-outer with multiple perspectives was growing. Grace feared losing something by gaining something – to see things with more complexity stimulated more growth and she wondered how she would relate to what was left behind – if she left herself behind to find herself ahead. Growing is filled with surprises. As for me, our sitting looking at each other was already feeling different. We were growing together.

Do you know Marion Milner's (1969) book, *The Hands of the Living God*? It is about long-term therapy with a woman patient Milner calls Susan, who is psychotic and an artist. Milner includes many of Susan's drawing in this book and therapy. If I remember, Susan may have been in therapy with Winnicott first and ended up with Milner, an artist as well. Linking inside-outside is one of the problems that interested Milner, something imperative in Susan's state. For example, what felt real to Susan might seem unreal in the outside world. If she shared something inwardly meaningful to her she might get a blank stare; puzzlement; incomprehension; or, worse, a look that signaled something wrong with her. Resonance between inner-outer was in jeopardy. With Milner's help Susan's use of art began to connect inner-outer realities, enriched by developing new connections. It is frightening how disconnected inner-outer can be or seem to be when in fact they are mutually permeable, inclusive as well as exclusive, depending on state, capacity, context.

Grace, too, was a kind of experiential artist, experimenting with linking inside-outside and how they work together. At one point she made the discovery that *feeling* new isn't *being* new. She could feel born again, a new beginning, transformed. And in a few minutes newness ebbs and she is just plain her back again. She has to get used to a sense of being born new and being just plain her.

I think of change of states Anton Ehrenzweig (1971), a friend of Milner's, describes in phases of creative processes. He depicts the artist feeling like God one moment, everything opens, comes together. Feeling, like Rabbi Nachman, no one ever painted like this before. In love with, intoxicated by his work. A little later he may look at what he thought was great and it seems like shit – how could he ever imagine it was wonderful. It was the most terrible thing he ever saw and wants to rip it up, throw it out. Ehrenzweig cautioned and advised, "Don't throw it out, don't rip it up. Let it sit. Stay with it. More will happen." Picasso would sit and stare at an unfinished piece that stalled for hours, days, until the work said "Do this" and something happened. Creative waiting is important in the self, personality, being of a person coming together too.

With coaching or self-coaching one begins to learn to tolerate swings of states between I am God and I am shit and lots more. In her own way, Grace is like this too. Sitting, looking at her torn and shattered life, staring at her being or sitting with me and sharing what she was seeing and feeling, talking about her way of experiencing, bringing it into the room, looking at her life, waiting for it to speak to her, waiting for her life to come together and say, "Now do this." And we sit quietly with her life, appreciating it together. We can feel her life looking at, sensing us, getting ready for the next moment.

Afternoon: gestation beyond symptoms

Andy Statman, a Brooklyn composer and musician, plays his clarinet each year at Rabbi Nachman's grave in Breslov, Ukraine. I have often felt a transmission from the Rabbi's spirit through Statman's music. It is not simply Nachman's spirit but a Godly spirit through him.

A Godly spirit that can be transmitted in many forms and registers, including psychosis. I remember the first time I heard the aphorism, "There are no atheists in foxholes." I was a little boy during World War II with strong imagination in many areas. When I boarded what seemed an abandoned boat near my home on the Passaic River, and touched with sacred puzzlement the torn canvas on the masts, I was certain it was a spy ship and searched for signs of enemy radio equipment. Little did I know my preoccupation with communication would become a lifelong calling. Is war a kind of universal or near-universal psychosis, objectifying terrors that have no names within?

And what about psychosis as a link to God, e.g., the case of Daniel Paul Schreber, a judge hospitalized three times who wrote persuasively about his psychotic states. Although he was never Freud's patient, Freud wrote a compelling account of Schreber's journey based on reading Schreber's memoir (Eigen, 1986 Chapter 7). Schreber transmitted one of the most alive and fascinating autobiographies of psychotic states. He felt he was perceiving the ultimate reality of things and had nerve to nerve contact with God. He was first hospitalized after a big promotion to the judgeship, apparently success triggering dread, in this case psychotic proportions. Freud pointed out difficulties inherent in success as well as failure. I've talked about Jim Henson's getting sick and dying when he sold the rights to Kermit, his alter ego. One wonders what role huge success played in Steve Job's early end from illness. One is almost brought to tears of awe by his last words, "Oh Wow! Oh Wow!", the amazing beauty of a difficult life well lived as best one can. Too much – too little, the effects of either or their combinations present intricacies for much thought and research.

Schreber's other breaks were triggered by deaths of his wife and mother. Some feel his megalomaniac delusions compensated for loss, God filling the place where emotional contact had been. Perhaps a parallel to the god-sized hole alcohol fills according to Alcoholics Anonymous. Schreber felt by becoming God's woman he kept God's interest in the universe alive and should he falter in his role, God would let go of creation and all would end. Quite a messianic role for a man to carry. In addition to sex change and reversal, Schreber introduced the term soul-murder into psychiatric lore. Indeed, soul murder and the task of keeping God alive were often fused. His descriptions of relationships with his asylum caretakers are rich with psychic journeys and complexities we can still mine today. As Freud said, we can learn a lot from psychotic individuals about what goes on inside us. With the help of our patients and many devoted workers psychic realities keep opening and we develop our own sensibilities. Today many workers would not be fazed if someone walks in talking about soul-murder. Ah, soul-murder, tell me more. Macbeth, speaking about Lady Macbeth's madness, asked the physician, "Canst thou not administer to a mind diseased?" The physician replied that he could not, the patient would have to cure herself. Bion added the physician might have said, "Come back in 200 years and we'll see what we can do." And we are trying.

It sounds like Schreber's life was sadder than Nachman's, although Schreber lived thirty years longer. Nachman died in his thirties like Luria and Jesus. Yet Schreber, a diagnosed psychiatric patient who wrote a book about his illness as a way to fight for his freedom, has had his own impact on future generations, including the one writing the words you are now reading. So many good people doing so many good things – there is danger of forgetting this, too, is a basic part of our lives.

Earlier today I was talking about a kind of manic-depressive rhythm in creative work, at least for many. Ehrenzweig's depictions of swings from "I am God – this is wonderful, look how good it is," to "This is awful – nothing good. Shit." An artist may go through both moments over and over. A positive aspect of extreme states is the role they can play in creativity. One has to swing with it, make room for change and development. Taoism speaks of the mind as a swinging door – our hinges have to be kept in good repair. No accident "unhinged" is another word for emotional variation, including madness. We can speak of the madness of everyday life. The doors of the psyche have capacity to swing many ways.

Often a key to work with a symptom is to find its positive function and support the personality to grow into it. Very often symptoms, like primary words, work opposite ways at once and force us to reach deeper levels of being. There are moments, too, when one tries to help symptoms find better ways of achieving what they are trying to do. Lacan feels symptoms are like umbilical cords, a basic part of personality. It may be giving expression to a heart of one's being. One uses the symptom as a clue, a path, a way back to the heart of one's being. We can make better contact with ourselves if we can realize its intent in a fuller way. Symptoms may be calling attention to a state of affairs that need our partnership and helping hand. What state of affairs is calling for attention?

When someone comes in and says, "Make my symptoms go away. Make me better." A symptom might say,

> If I vanish just like that you might miss an important part of your life. I'm here to stir you up, find something. It's understandable to want to be rid of pain, guilt, anxiety, bad functioning, bad feelings. But there is a state of affairs aching to be heard and worked with. There may be more to you than you imagine, not just the less you feel because of me.

> I don't want you to lose out on something in yourself by assigning it to oblivion. I want to help you find some bit of the state of affairs you were in before I came. I'm here to protect you, not just harm and do you in.

During our first day I spoke of a patient's arm falling off dream that Bion reported. The patient wanted his arm to do something, signal danger, but instead the arm fell off. It did not want to do what the patient told it to. Let me make up a little interchange. "Why did you fall off?" I say to my arm and my arm might say, "I didn't want to follow your directions." I could add a lot of "not wants":

> I didn't want to practice piano two hours a day, I didn't want to get an A on a test you studied so hard for, I didn't want to hit the ball you tried to hit, I didn't want to do what you wanted me to do...

"So what do you want, arm? What would make it possible for you not to fall off?"

I am learning to begin a dialogue with my arm to see what it wants and why it is so opposed to what I want. Pierre Janet did something like this with a hospitalized patient who was being ruled by a devil. He began a dialogue asking the devil what it wanted. Little by little we learn to talk with our symptoms and learn more about them, more about what they are there for, their role, function, aim, desire. A symptom disguises and points to something existentially wrong. You can't just say, "All right, let's get rid of you somehow." The symptom is objecting to our way of life. It's saying,

> I don't want you to be living this way. I'm not going to go away. I want something more, something different to happen. If you want me to diminish, you are going to have to make a change that you need to make.

A symptom may have its reason. One has to expand to make room for the symptom and engage its alarm. Is it an accident of language that alarm has arm in it, that Bion's patient's arm falling off dream is like an alarm system? One has to grow, needs to grow. Telling a symptom to go away is like telling yourself to go away, I don't want to listen to you, it's just too much trouble and I don't know how. My "I" is a symptom, my "self" is a symptom, and I want to make it all go away. But the hard work is to try to make it more dialogical, let conversations between the different parts grow. I remember a patient who was starting to catch on say, "This may sound strange but in a way my symptoms might be more ethical than the rest of me." He was beginning to feel symptoms were like guardians telling him he was doing something wrong to his life.

They could be saying, "If you live a fuller, different way, a more open way I won't have to be here so much."

QUESTION 1: What about the feeling whatever we do we will ruin it? Whether we ask or don't ask we will be stuck. If we have a patient who has been stuck for a long, long time, what can we do? What kind of attitude can help?

RESPONSE 1: If you are stuck this long a time, maybe you can stick it out even longer. I remember, too, a patient of Bion saying he was thinking of leaving because he hadn't changed a bit in the twelve years they were working together and Bion replied, "Do you mind telling me how you did that?" Change is part of life, even in the seemingly unchanging. Elizabeth Sewell would speak of changes a rock would make over time in texture, coloration, contours in response to wind, sunlight, temperature. What kinds of changes can one notice in the changeless and unchangeable? When speaking about "repetition dreams," Gregory Bateson would ask what "news of difference" could be detected.

QUESTION 2: Grace seemed to feel stuck and not stuck at the same time. She seemed to be flooded by intersubjective sensations yet deeply alone too. You seemed receptive to both poles as they rose and fell. Can you comment?

RESPONSE 2: On the one hand, everything is intersubjective in human relations. If you pretend we are not intersubjective that is intersubjective too. Pretense is strong self-other engagement. Sometimes I speak of a distinction-union structure, both poles part of every psychic act. Lacan's tri-un psychic structure, the imaginary-symbolic-real, also contains tensions and fusions between multiple poles. We are made of paradoxes. For example, deeply alone and linked – again a turn of language, alone, all-one.

Winnicott tries to bring out that for the baby even aloneness has to be supported by the unknown other. The baby may not know that support is there or what it is but it is important to be there or the deficiency would be overwhelming. Without it there could not be good quality aloneness, even the latter needs support.

We have all worked with people who cannot be alone. Sometimes it is linked with too much symbiosis early in life but more often lack of intersubjective support is at work. If aloneness is felt as toxic one has to create closeness-distance balances that help support personality. Good quality aloneness needs good quality intersubjectivity.

Being with Grace or someone like Grace one goes through a lot of different interactions. Often I may be a background presence, a presence that has resonance, that vibrates in the room but is in some way unobtrusive. At such moments the patient feels her words are not falling into a void on deaf ears. A sense of being heard adds tone, texture, atmospheric resonance rather than drifting into space. I think I'm using the word intersubjective because you used it in your question. Intrapsychic can work too, psyche-to-psyche. To feel one's words held by a wordless response. One can say more, one can say less, but a response is in the quiet of the room.

When I was a little boy at a circus I saw a magician cut up a lady in a box and at the end of the act she would jump out of the box all together, whole. A situation that models so many moments of being in bits and pieces, cut up, lost forever, then whole again, just plain me, a drama our insides go through throughout our lifetime. All the ways of cutting up reality and piecing it together. In Day 2 I spoke about work of Matte-Blanco and David Bohm showing ways reality divides itself up and puts itself together. Reality supports so many positions and perspectives, proverbial hands on the elephant, many maps but no one map for the whole.

Qualities of intersubjectivity undergo so many moment to moment changes, one never knows when a hole will open up and one will fall through. Someone in Grace's position has to learn over time with her therapist to go through scores of states and negotiate bad feelings, making room for "the wrong" and not having to keep going to the hospital for recovery. Both partners learn how to tolerate the therapy relationship itself, a learning that goes on and on, building more tolerance for being a person. One begins to take in that the challenge of being human is an insistent part of existence (Eigen, 2018).

Therapy is like a gymnasium, we practice going through things together until we build up better habits of feeling and talking about them to another human being. Faith grows, as in the psalm, Yea though I walk through the valley of death, You are with me. It may not be clear who the You is or how it works, but it makes a difference. Going through, over and over. I'd like to add coming through, never perfectly, always flawed, but it makes a difference.

QUESTION 3: What can we do?

RESPONSE 3: What particular problems and organizations does "we" mean in a particular instance? Bion would say if you think you are seeing the same patient you're seeing the wrong patient. One would have to become acquainted with the particulars. We may all share basic qualities but we are also unique. Each moment of work is a discovery. Living in not knowing makes for a certain humility and openness. Sometimes I call it the Way of Unknowing, an approach with ancient roots and current advocates. Both Bion and Theodore Reik talked about the importance of surprise in our work. Bion added beauty. There is beauty as well as danger making contact with the unknown psyche. But it may be even more dangerous not to.

In work with psychosis you may not perceive changes for a long, long time, but that does not mean that nothing is happening. In certain instances it can take ten, fifteen years for changes to become perceptible. This sounds like a terrible thing in an age where so much is rushed.

Because baby is not born immediately after fertilization does not mean something important is not happening in months of gestation. In the domain of psychosis and wounded dependency years of gestation could be like a day. At this point in my life I have a number of patients who have been with me forty or fifty years. You might think this not possible in an age of insurance dictates or not desirable in itself. Yet we have been growing older together and the needed support for existence has made a difference for survival and quality of being. Each life has its own trajectories and seeing what is possible is part of self-discovery.

One learns that something underneath the "symptoms" can be undergoing changes. It is possible that the same symptom can take on different meanings and functions at different times, in part depending on how deeper underlying processes are working. A kind of dialectic of creative waiting, patience, and impatience moves along the edge of experience opening dimensions of being as we go.

Frustration, too, can be an important link and, at times, a part of growth. In my book Rage (2002, p. 25), I put something along these lines more dramatically: "One must not underestimate gains that come from an ever-growing education in futility." There are moments when frustration and a more extreme state of futility can be a link between yourself and another and also between you and yourself.

I'm thinking of a case in which a person's (let's call him Ben) frustration with himself turned out to have significant reference to his parents' impatient frustration with him as a baby. He remembers his mother, especially, in his earliest years being beside herself with housework and baby-work. She had not realized it would be so hard to calm a crying baby and could not deal with the fact that her own nervous impatience increased Ben's discomfort. She just did not have a natural feel for comforting a baby and had all she could do to try to comfort herself. As Ben grew his father added his anger to the mother's anxiety and between parental anger-anxiety Ben was lost and at a loss to find his own center. The pain of existence spiraled.

As our work went on Ben began to feel that he was addicted to the pain, frustration, and anger and that relationships that were calm and giving did not appeal. He seemed to need the intensity of pain-anger-anxiety as a kind link, a frustration link. That was part of what bound him to his parents, a kind of aversive bond, a negative thread of attachment that had a strong hold. Yet he stayed in therapy as a life-raft and in time increasingly valued the calmer and calming atmosphere of our being together, as if our work was building an alternative reality that offset a sense of damage. For years self-damaging activity would make him feel whole and now he began to feel and speak about the gap it filled, the gap of a more calming love together with supportive-stimulating interchanges. It was a world of feeling that ached to be found and grow.

What do you do with a baby? Baby and parent can feel helpless with each other, neither knowing what to do with the other. Some of this helplessness can be transferred to the therapist. If it becomes too intense and frustrating it may even provoke a wish on the part of the therapist to get rid of the patient. The patient becomes someone the therapist does not want to be with as well as feeling he does not know what to do or how to help. The perception may dawn that it is better to have a frustrating link than no link at all. But over time awareness deepens as one reaches for ways better feeling can displace, be added to, or offset the bad. New links can grow.

A variation may involve the patient learning how to modulate frustration in the room so that the therapist continues working. One discovers a kind of art in maintaining the frustration level in a way so that one does not have to change yet does not provoke the therapist to end the therapy. There are many balancing acts in life and therapy between contrary tendencies. I may look like I'm about to change, then go back to status quo, so that a certain range of frustration remains my link with the other, with the world, a kind of lifelong umbilical cord. Will I ever tire of this kind of lifeline or are the dangers too great without it? How does one go about finding out what else is possible?

Sometimes it takes facing death for doors to open. I'm thinking of a patient who has terminal cancer and who may die any week or month. Coming to therapy seems to give her a little more time or way to use her time. She said, "When I have a dream I feel like God is seeing me." As she spoke I felt us both deepening. She did not have many dreams and when she did she felt happy that God did not forget her. She tried to describe a part of what the dream felt like to her.

> I feel God is saying, 'This is what you look and feel like to me. If I would paint a picture of you, this is what it would be - your dream.' I never was able to put into words the depth of a dream. This is as close as I've come. I don't have time not to say it now. I don't have time not to say what I want to say, especially to myself. It sounds awful to say but I don't think I'd reach this depth if I didn't have cancer.

In a way she was saying that reaching this depth helps her handle the cancer.

In another instance a strong, athletic woman learned that her neighbor, a young woman like herself, had cancer and was expected to die within a year. Unexpectedly, she was plunged into a state of extreme pain. She could not believe this woman, with a son the same age as her own son, was going to die. The two boys played together all the time. When she saw the two boys playing with each other across the yard she felt unbearable pain. She was in tears and did not know what to do with the pain. She never felt this way before. She had managed to pass by or somehow modulate pain this intense. Then another surprise – when she was watching the boys play the pain turned into extreme joy – extreme pain and extreme joy. Joy of life continuing, pain of life ending. She was overcome by feeling and looked to me for help. I encouraged her to stay with it, let it open. She focused more on her son and felt he was showing her something, teaching her, pulling out a precious feeling she didn't know she could feel, a whole new feeling world. She said, "I'm fearful. Growth is so painful. I can't believe I'm saying this but I'm feeling a kind of faith. Faith in a spontaneous moment that can pull something out of you, teach you, show you."

A patient read a sentence in *The Sensitive Self* (2004) that stayed with her: "In an important way we remain embryonic, unborn, premature and immature all our days." The sentence touched something unexpectedly and she found herself expressing a yearning for more communal sharing of unborn-ness. As I felt her ache and wish I began to see how important it was to find a communal way of sharing our brokenness and our unborn, embryonic state. I felt for moments my patient and I contacted a shared way we are whole, broken, embryonic. I felt we were communicating embryo to embryo.

QUESTION 4: The other day (Day 1) you spoke of Levinas's writings about the face and I think of him in these accounts of being opened by death and incompletion at the same time as being unborn and embryonic. Can you say more about the ethics of the face?

RESPONSE 4: Levinas was, for me, a very deeply moving writer. He came from Lithuania and settled in Paris. He was an officer in the French army in World War II, captured by the Germans and spent the rest of the war in an officer's camp. After the war he eventually taught in a girl's school in Paris where there is a tiny square now called "Levinas Square."

In my reading, he contrasted totality and infinity (1969). Totalizing thinking is a kind of absolutism meaning what it sounds like: "total" – this is it, all of it. He felt totalizing viewpoints helped lead to war. My view is right and all there is. If we each feel that way about our viewpoints fighting takes the place of dialogue. If we are aware that our views are partial and incomplete, humility may take the place of absolutism. As with infinity, there is more to go. In my written work, you can find discussions of Levinas in *The Electrified Tightrope* (1993) and *Emotional Storm* (2005).

In a couple of days I am going to Busan for the First World Humanities Forum sponsored by the United Nations. Many thinkers, writers, scientists, visionaries, and activists will be there. We will be talking about what the humanities can contribute to working with world problems, on what human beings share, and seeing if there is any path towards a more peaceful world. For me this is an astonishing event and

I am sure Levinas would be pleased by a multiplicity of approaches trying to understand our predicament. Maybe nothing will come of it. Maybe it will be useless. But the fact that there is going to be such an event I find hopeful. There are so many pockets under the radar trying to do something good for the world. Bits here, there, often outside the mainstream, trying to make the world a better place. We haven't given up on it. What are the possibilities that violent creatures like us who totalize perspectives can somehow find our way to a more peaceful existence valuing aspects of what all humanity shares?

Levinas contrasts a closed, totalizing-totalitarian attitude with infinity, an open attitude. One way we experience the human face from infancy on is vulnerable, naked, infinite, arousing an urge to do justice to the other. The other's expressive face calls to us and we need to respond or find a response that does the call justice. In this regard, one of Levinas's phrases is "Ethics is an optics." The expressive face of the other awakens us to who we are, our call to care, to do justice to life. As we know, this is not our only attitude, but Levinas traces it as a valued thread, an essential part of our being, a call to deeply felt truth.

Research by psychologists intersect with Levinas's account of the experience of the face. Elkin (1972) uses some of this research to elaborate a theory about the importance of the face in early development. He describes emotional dramas in which the face plays a central role and contributes to the growth of the human. For Levinas, there are ways the face takes us to God and Elkin has a parallel to that in early primordial self-other dramas. For Levinas, even though we can't possibly exhaust or perfectly fulfill our responsibility to the other, what we offer no one else can give. We have our own special gift of self-giving.

The naked vulnerability of the face and our call to respond carries a critique of life insofar as living out our life drive kills and injures. The ethical call of the face stands opposed to the assertion of our vitality in disregard of the other. My life drive, desire, may want more territory, want what you have, but the ethics of the face critiques it. I cannot injure you just because you stand in my way and your path conflicts with mine. A power drive may conflict with responsibility towards the other. A will to live, will to power can disregard the life of others in order to get what I want. There are ways an ethics of the face and life drive may conflict. The face says, "Don't kill me, don't hurt me. Talk with me, be with me, care."

Conflicts between love and power are ancient and by no means simple. What do we do with our will to power? What do we do with our lust, our desires that run over the other? We don't know what. We have not solved it. The state of the world shows us we have not solved it. Perhaps more evolution is required together with learning how to partner ourselves and our capacities. Levinas raises the question but there is a long way to go. The face and its infinite call asks for response that requires more growth.

In part, Levinas's philosophy is a response to the mass murders of World War II. How could people do this to each other, a question still being asked today in different contexts. And we, or some of us, are trying to face it to the extent we can. The human race has a division of labor, not everyone doing the same thing. For example, Buddhist emphasis on emptiness contrasts with King David's emotionality in the psalms, one moment filled with the Divine Presence, another abandoned, another singing and dancing. Both paths are important threads of our being and working with them increases psycho-spiritual resources.

Levinas is a specialist in what one might call an allocentric as opposed to autocentric viewpoint. We are self-centered and other-centered and need to learn how to make them work well together, so that we become less destructive. Instead of splitting them and totalizing one against the other we can try to learn how they can contribute in creative and useful ways. Appreciate what different people are trying to do with the equipment at hand. No one can be a specialist in all human tendencies. We need each other to supplement and add to what any of us can do.

Levinas has poetic, wondrous, philosophical writings. His allocentric view is more than not doing to others what you would not want done to you. The other calls to me, an infinite call, and I have to respond in an infinite way. There is no end to my response to the call from the other. It is beyond anything I can possibly do as a human being yet it makes me more human. He brings this dimension of life alive, a very important dimension balanced by others. But he touches with particular beauty and care our challenge and need to serve each other.

QUESTION 5: This is more of a request than a question. Two years ago you came and talked about a trauma deep inside us and how that trauma never really disappears. But our psyche grows so the space that the trauma takes up grows smaller. This gave me a deep sense of relief. Now whenever someone comes to me who has severe trauma, who has not died, who has not gone crazy, I feel very grateful. Can you please – for me and for those who come to me – can you please make a short prayer for us.

RESPONSE 5: Let us be silent together.

[After some time feeling and becoming the silence]
Lord, help us keep opening.
I think of Winnicott's prayer, "Lord, let me be alive when I die."
We will change the prayer a little bit... Lord, help us be alive while we live. Help us keep opening. Help us. Help us keep opening.

* * *

Here is a vignette about a woman who has been through a lot. I wrote about her in the chapter "Alone With God" in *The Sensitive Self* (2004), a woman who was supposed to die nine years ago. In a recent session she was talking about her family in her early childhood. Her mother became ill and died when the patient and she both were very young. Yet it took time for death-work to happen as her body deteriorated slowly. Her mother had to live in a small setting next to the main house so she could get the undisturbed care and attention needed.

The mother's caretaker and sister were afraid of my patient being close to her mother, partly to shield the little girl from seeing the mother's terrible condition. In my patient's words,

> The suffering of the household was denied. My mother was in a little house next to the main house and the household pretended it wasn't happening. They did not want me to know about it, see it. Then a strange thing began to happen and in a way continues to his day. Because suffering was denied I began to think the good parts of being alive were lies too. It looked like everyone was lying about what was going on so that good things started to look phony. After all, not all good things are really good things. Not all good things are real.

Something to think about. If the suffering was denied, if the bad was denied, since the truth was denied, the good stated to look like a lie.

* * *

I'm told the case I want to talk about now was translated into Korean and handed out, the chapter "Tears of Pain and Beauty: Mixed Voices" from *Contact With the Depths* (2011). This morning I met the man who translated it, Kim, and we spoke. I don't want to put you on the spot, Kim, but I'd love it if you can say a few words about your experience of translating the piece. Would you honor us with a few words about your experience?

KIM: It was a great honor to be given an opportunity to translate this case about a man called Kurt and how he contends and deals with psychosis and psychotic transformations. At times it was hard for me to follow, but I appreciated how the therapy work gave him very deep insight and was a very precious journey of recovery. Translating it brought what he went through closer to me and when I thank you for the opportunity of doing this I feel Kurt thanking you too.

MIKE: Thank you too, Kim. More than happy!

This case is about – like Grace – a man who suffered multiple hospitalizations and a lot of medication. When I met him he was taking five medications. After twelve years of therapy, he was hospital- and medication-free. Not all patients I see become medication free – it depends what is needed and works at particular times. You all have the translation of "Tears of Pain and Beauty" so no need for me to read it. Let me say what comes to me now about our work and we'll see how it goes.

At first we had trouble connecting. He would call and I wouldn't get the number right. I tried reaching him but it would be the wrong number or he hung up or would speak so quickly I could not understand him. Likewise, he spoke so fast in messages he left I could not make out what he was saying. Then by some stroke of luck, like playing a slot machine, the numbers came up right and we made contact and set up an appointment.

When it was time for his appointment no one rang or came in so I went to the door and looked out. No one was there. I went back in and waited some more, then felt drawn to the door and opened it again and there he was. I wondered if he couldn't make up his mind about coming in or not or was simply in a fairly usual state of semi-paralysis.

He couldn't say why he couldn't come in but let me know he had an urge to run out of the building, out to the street, where he'd feel safe. Walking was one of the things he liked to do, walking all over the city. I began to get the idea my office was too confining, scary. Then he looked at me sternly, straight in the face and said over and over, "The simplest kind of proposition, an elementary proposition, asserts the existence of a state of affairs."

I assumed everything he was doing was a form of contact – not coming in, leaving obscure messages, going back and forth, wanting to run away. Not making contact was a form of contact. I knew where the quote was from but did not tell him I knew. I just sat with the existence of a state of affairs and in my mind a state of affairs he was asserting was that of his existential dilemma, his existential traumatic position.

I had been a Wittgenstein reader (Eigen, 2005) and recognized the proposition from the *Tractatus* (1998). Wittgenstein had his own difficulties and I could readily understand Kurt's resonance to him. If I were, perhaps a normal therapist or person, I might think Kurt intellectualized, defending against feeling, and I can't judge whether that is or is not so or how. But I did feel his sensitivity communicating through Wittgenstein as a mouthpiece – words at last. Pretty abstract, out of world maybe, but I'm in some sense crazy too and take the communication. He is communicating the existence of a state of affairs – his existence. I am thinking he is doing very well, the best he can do this moment and he pushed himself to do it, channeling Wittgenstein to speak for him and his dilemma. Responding to his assertion of his existence I say, "You are here."

Later I learn the words "You are here" were threatening and relieving. Therapy was potentially violating. He fear being robbed of himself. He could see people walking back and forth outside the window of my office and that gave him some sense of relief. He could leave, escape. If his feet carry him he does not have to be stuck. One reason he likes walking so much. After a while, he looks at me and says, "You know I can't be here." I thought he was going to cry. Going into my office felt like going inside a cage. I was thinking I also have a tendency to stop short, leave. But I also have a sticky side. Run, stay – who knows? It's not easy to be with another person and not easy to be alone.

Inside the outer room of my office is a door to the consulting room. I saw Kurt taking in the situation, then lean towards the inner door ever so slightly, and I automatically began to lean with him. We both were leaning when he said, "Thank you."

We don't have time to do much more now but you have the paper. You might call our work together, Kurt and I, you and me, an act of faith. How close, how far, with what tools of approach and avoidance, towards-away. Kurt went through many stages of recovery. My office is across the street from Central Park, the main park of the city and for a time he began sleeping in it. Again a mixture of free and confined. Leaving me began to feel like too much separation and being with me felt like too little. For some time the park felt just right. He could view my office when taking a walk.

Another phase was watching movies for hours. The darkened theater was comforting as well as confining and looking at the movies was like looking at his mind, one waking dream after another. He was getting closer to himself while keeping enough distance to make more closeness possible. He began to think of making movies himself.

The years went by and he kept finding more areas of freedom, areas he could move in, work with. He had to deal with the Commands of a Negative Voice that he was learning to turn into a movie character, the principle of Evil. It was not easy but he was exercising himself, working with the psyche and its age-old problems. Now it was his turn. We will leave him for now working with voices and images, threats and passageways, finding a partner, on the verge of becoming a father. How did this happen? There is life in us, strange life, beauty and horror, and having someone who can help us become a better partner to ourselves makes a difference. I know that time can be an enemy, but for some of us, many of us, time can become a partner telling us its secrets while remaining a mystery. And we recognize these secrets as our own. Meanwhile, we continue gestating.

References

Bion, W. R. (1965). *Transformations*. London: Routledge.
——— (1970). *Attention and Interpretation*. Lanham, MD: Rowman & Littlefield 1995.
——— (1978). *The Paris Seminar*. Transcribed and Ed. F. Bion. http://braungardt.trialectics.com/projects/psychoanalysis/bion/seminar-in-paris/
——— (1991). *A Memoir of the Future*. London: Routledge.
——— (1994). *Cogitations*. Ed. F. Bion. London: Routledge.
Bion, W. R. (1970). *Attention and Interpretation*. Lanham, MD: Jason Aronson, 1995.
Bohm, D. (2002). *Wholeness and the Implicate Order*. London: Routledge.
Buber, M. (1937). *I and Thou*. New York: Simon and Schuster.
Castaneda, C. (1969). *Teachings of Don Juan: A Yaqui Way of Knowledge*. New York: Washington Square Press.
Chuang Tzu (1964). *Chuang Tzu: Basic Writings*. Tr. B. Watson. New York: Columbia University Press.
Ehrenzweig, A. (1971). *The Hidden Order of Art*. Berkeley: University of California Press.
Eigen, M. (1996). *Psychic Deadness*. London: Routledge.
——— (1979). On the Significance of the Face. *The Psychoanal. Rev.* 67: 427–442. Collected in The Electrified Tightrope (1993).
——— (1986). *The Psychotic Core*. London: Routledge.
——— (1993). *The Electrified Tightrope*. Ed. A. Phillips. London: Routledge.
——— (1998). *The Psychoanalytic Mystic*. London: Free Association Books.
——— (2002). *Rage*. Middletown, CT: Wesleyan University Press.
——— (2004). *The Sensitive Self*. Middletown, CT: Wesleyan University Press.
——— (2005). *Emotional Storm*. Middletown, CT: Wesleyan University Press.
——— (2006). Something wrong. Online in *Moondance*. http://www.moondance.org/2006/summer2006/fiction/wrong.html
——— (2007). *Feeling Matters*. London: Routledge.
——— (2009). *Flames from the Unconscious: Trauma, Madness and Faith*. London: Routledge.
——— (2010). *Eigen in Seoul vol. 1: Madness and Murder*. London: Routledge.
——— (2011a). *Eigen in Seoul vol. 2: Faith and Transformation*. London: Routledge.
——— (2011b). *Contact with the Depths*. London: Routledge,
——— (2012). *Kabbalah and Psychoanalysis*. London: Routledge.
——— (2014a). *Faith*. London: Routledge.

——— (2014b). *The Birth of Experience*. London: Routledge.
——— (2018). *The Challenge of Being Human*. London: Routledge.
Elkin, H. (1972). On Selfhood and the Development of Ego Structures in Infancy. *The Psychoanal. Rev.* 59: 389–416. Collected in *The Origin of the Self: The Collected Papers of Henry Elkin*. Ed. L. Daws. Solana Beach, CA: Epis Publishing Co, 2016.
Fliees, R. 1973 *Symbol, Dream and Psychosis*. New York: International Universities Press.
Green, A. (1975). The Analyst, Symbolization and Absence in the Analytic Setting (on Changes in Analytic Practice and Analytic Experience). *Int J Psychol Psychoanal.* 56: 1–22.
——— (1999). *The Work of the Negative*. London: Free Association Books.
Gurwitsch, A. (1964). *The Field of Consciousness*. Pittsburgh: Duquesne University Press.
Levinas, E. (1969). *Totality and Infinity*. Pittsburgh: Duquesne University Press.
Márquez, G. G. (1967). *One Hundred Years of Solitude*. New York: Harpers Perennials.
Matte-Blanco, I. (1975). *The Unconscious as Infinite Sets: An Essay in Bi-logic*. London: Routledge.
——— (1980). *Thinking, Feeling and Being: Clinical Reflections on the Fundamental Antinomy of Human Beings in the World*. London: Routledge.
Meltzer, D. (1973). *Sexual States of Mind*. London: Roland Harris Trust.
Milner, M. (1969). *The Hands of the Living God: An Account of a Psychoanalytic Treatment*. London: Routledge.
Perls, F. (1992). *Gestalt Therapy Verbatim*. Gouldsboro, ME: Gestalt Journal Press.
Tatarsky, A. (2007). *Harm Reduction Therapy*. Lanham, MD: Jason Aronson
Trasntromer, T. (2006). *The Great Enigma: New Collected Poems*. Tr. R. Fulton. New York: New Directions Books.
Winnicott, D. W. (1974). Fear of breakdown. *Int. Rev. Psycho-Anal.* 1: 103–107.
Wittgenstein, L. (1998). *Tractatus Logico-Philosphicus*. Tr. C. K. Ogden. Mineola, NY: Dover Books.
Zalman, S. (1779, 2020). *Likkutei Amarim: Tanya*. Brooklyn, NY: Kehot Publication Society.

Index

affective attitudes 7, 13, 19, 22, 33–34
aggression 22, 72
Akiva (Rabbi) 2, 43–45, 47, 58
Alcoholics Anonymous 76
antiquity 42, 46
anxiety 30, 31; catastrophic 29
arm falling off dream 22–23, 29, 33, 36, 78
asymmetrical consciousness 56, 63
asymmetrical thinking 54–55
Attention and Interpretation (Bion) 39
attitude 7, 22; affective 7, 13, 19, 22, 33–34; psychoanalytic 49; totalizing-totalitarian 84

Baal Shem Tov 57, 58, 65
Bateson, Gregory 79
beauty 50, 52
Bergson, Henri 55
"Be still. Listen and know God" 41
Bible 6, 29, 42, 62–64
Big Bang 66
bina 50
Bion, W. R. 1, 2, 8, 12, 19, 40, 47, 55, 58, 68, 73, 80; advantages of having love and hate 54; appealed to faith 43; arm falling off dream 22–23, 29, 33, 36, 78; arm signaling distress 29; *Attention and Interpretation* 39; bewildered patient 28; describes psychoanalysis 13; desire to help 30; difficulties of common sense 33–34; emotions for adults 20; fundamental psychic reality 48; hyper-development of capacities 21–22; maximum-minimum emotion 36–38; patient's dream 23–26, 30, 32; permeability and evacuation 14–15; psychic catastrophe 66; psychotic state 38–39; references to Saint John of the Cross 55; sense of foundational infinity 64; work and Kabbalah 52
bio-psycho-spiritual image 63
Blake, William 27, 72
Bloom, Harold 51
Bohm, David 56, 80
Buber, M.: I and Thou 21
Buddha 62–63, 65
Buddhism 49
bumping into oneself 2, 4–22

capacity: emotional incapacity 19; hyper-development of 21–22; typologies of 67; under-used 21; use of 21–22; to work with dreams 19, 35
Carlyle, Thomas 41
Castaneda, Carlos 34
Chassidic communities 57
Chesed 50
chochma 49–50
Chuang-Tzu 44, 49
conflict 53, 56, 73; between love and power 84; between psychic democracy and psychic tyrannies 28; with responsibility 84
constant conjunction 25, 33
constant struggle 64
Contact with the Depths (Eigen) 13, 31, 86–88
control: gesture of 11; ideology of 10–11; model of 12

desire to help 30
destruction 66, 69–71, 85
distinction-union structure 2, 53, 54, 57, 79; balance and off-balance in 61
divine energy 48, 50, 51

dream 2, 8–9; arm falling off 22–23, 29, 33, 36, 78; dreamer portrays catastrophe 26; elements of 18; experiences outside of reach 17; fragments of 13; narrative structure 15–16; scary 8; semi-narrative processes 16; successful 9; trying to communicate 32–33
dreamless sleep 17, 20, 21
dreamless void 17
dream work, importance of 15

Ehrenzweig, Anton 75, 77
Eigen, Michael: bumping into oneself 4–22; *Contact with the Depths* 13, 31, 86–88; *The Electrified Tightrope* 83; *Emotional Storm* 83; experience of being lost while alive 3; *Flames From the Unconscious: Trauma, Madness and Faith* 67; gestation beyond symptoms 76–88; heart, soul, and might 40–51; helpless against helplessness 22–39; hidden sparks 51–65; infinite psyche 2; *Kabbalah and Psychoanalysis* 42; miracles of everyday 66–75; *Moondance* 67; *The Psychotic Core* 52–53; *Rage* 11, 81; *The Sensitive Self* 62, 83, 86; "Something Wrong" 3, 67–75; *Toxic Nourishment* 32; value our psyche 1
Ein Sof 48–50
The Electrified Tightrope (Eigen) 83
Eliot, T.S. 61
Elkin, Henry 2, 54, 63, 84
Eloheinu 41
Emerson, Ralph Waldo 55
emotional irritants 8
emotional pain 7, 8, 19–20
emotional reality, in psychoanalysis 43
Emotional Storm (Eigen) 83
emotional transmissions 13–14
emotional violence 73
empowerment 67
Energy Eternal Delight 72
ethics 6, 84; of face 5

face: ethics of 5; nakedness of 5; vulnerability of 5, 84
faith 43–45, 48–49, 65
feeling: bad 68–69; discernment of 58; of prayer 65; psyche supports 11
First World Humanities Forum 83
Flames From the Unconscious: Trauma, Madness and Faith (Eigen) 67

Fliess, Robert 71
Fliess, Wilhelm 41, 71
forces: catastrophic anxiety 29; creative 27; degree of 27; destructive 15; that constitute lives through tensions 33; at work 30
Freud, Sigmund 2, 10, 15, 17, 22, 25, 30, 41, 46, 51, 59; emphasis on separation-identification 54; frustration of wishes 72–73; growing up stresses, psychosomatic system 27–28; patient journey 76; of reality testing 23
frozenness, qualities of 66
frustration 16, 57, 72–73, 81, 82

Garden of Eden 9, 25, 44–45, 70
George, Amanda 67
Gevurah 50
Gospel of Thomas 42
Greece 67
Green, Andre 37, 73

The Hands of the Living God? (Milner) 75
Hebrew 41, 45
helplessness 82; helpless against 22–39
Henson, Jim 37, 76
Hillel (Rabbi) 60
Hod 50–51
humanity 65, 84; living close to God and 57; suffering of 74

I and Thou (Buber) 21
impotence 24, 27, 29
impulse control 10–11
impulse, gap between action and 11, 12
infinite psyche 1; timelessness of 1–2
infinity 45, 48, 55, 64; totalizing-totalitarian attitude with 84
internal catastrophic explosion 66
International Forum for Psychoanalytic Education 67
"intimations of immortality" 55
intuition 43, 48, 51

Jae Hoon Lee 7
Jews 45, 57; mysticism 47; service 41
Job, Steve 76
Joon Ho 67
Joyce, James: *Ulysses* 41
Jung, Carl 2, 40, 51, 62, 63

Kabbalah 22, 40, 47, 52; mystical nature of 2; taste for hidden meanings 42

Kabbalah and Psychoanalysis (Eigen) 42
Kabbalah Tree of Life 42, 48, 49, 51
Kabbalistic numerology 41
Kafka 9
Kant, Immanuel 20, 21
kavanah 45
Khan, Masud 31
Kiefer, Anselm 51
King David 49, 64, 85
Klein, Melanie 15, 59
knowing-unknowing 64–65

Lacan, Jacques 77; tri-un psychic structure 79
de Leon, Moses 44, 46
Levinas, Emmanuel 5, 83, 84; response to mass murders of World War II 85
Luria (Rabbi) 51
Luria, Isaac 47, 48
Lurianic Kabbalah 52

madness 42, 45
Malchut 51
Malkut 66
manic-depressive rhythm 77
Márquez, Gabriel García 21
Matte-Blanco, Ignacio 2, 54–56, 63, 80; symmetrical unconscious 64
maximum-minimum emotion 36–38
Meltzer, D. 19, 55
Menachem Mendel of Kotzk (Rabbi) 59
Milner, Marion 49; *The Hands of the Living God?* 75
Molofsky, Merle 67
Moondance (Eigen) 67
Mozart, Wolfgang Amadeus 49–50
Muir, Edmond 4
multitudes 1, 3, 54
The Muppet Show 37

Nachman (Rabbi) 2, 34, 57, 59, 63, 70, 75–77; constant struggle 64; distinctionunion extremes 58; emptiness-fullness 61; knowing and not knowing 64–65; life as musical 63–64
narrative processes 15–16
National Psychological Association for Psychoanalysis 67
"negative twos" 28
negativism 66
Netzach 50–51
The New School 67

New York University Contemplative Studies Project 40
nineteenth-century psychology 34
numerology 41

open attitude 84

pain, of life 52
The Paris Seminar (Bion) 35
Pascal, Blaise 35
peace 4–5; tensions between civil strife and 28
periphery vision 1
personality 28, 32, 36–37; creative force in 27; elements of 34, 55; to fight against feeling an inhuman menace 69; male and female aspects of 41; part of 28, 29; sense of 28; tone of 14–15; typologies of 67
Plato 20, 21, 42
profound peace 4–5
profound sleep 4–5
psyche 15, 27, 72, 77; Big Bang of 47; blownup 38; evolution of 35–36; hidden meanings of 42; human spirit and 3; infinite 1–2; supports feeling 11; unhappiness for 28; value our 1
psychic catastrophe 52, 66
psychic plasticity 21
psychic toxins, tolerance for 7
psychoanalysis 7, 10, 12–13, 21, 30, 34; emotional irritants 8; emotional reality in 43; Kabbalah and 40; as "talking cure" 41; taste for hidden meanings 42
psychoanalytic attitude 49
psychoanalytic madness 42
psychosis 80–81
psychotherapy 8, 9, 21, 67
The Psychotic Core (Eigen) 52–53
psychotic explosion 35, 38
psychotic state 38–39

Rage (Eigen) 11, 81
reality: emotional 43; emotional in psychoanalysis 43; intuition of 43; testing of 23; unknown emotional 48–49; unknown ultimate 43, 49
Reik, Theodore 80
religion 6, 7, 10, 69, 71
resonance 48, 52; between inner-outer 75
Romans 43, 45
Roosevelt, Theodore 4, 6

sacred sense 7
Saint Paul 43
Satan Energy 72
scary dreams 8
Schneur Zalman (Rabbi) 58
Scholem, Gershom 47
Schreber, Daniel Paul 50, 76–77
self-hate 14, 71
sensation 43, 48, 51, 61
The Sensitive Self (Eigen) 62, 83, 86
sephirot 48, 50; structure of 51; and yoga chakras 49
Sephirotic Tree 48
Shabbos (Sabbath) candles 6–7
Shakespeare, William 37–38
Shimon bar Yochai (Rabbi) 43, 44, 46, 47
Singer, Elizabeth 67
sleep 4–5; dreamless 17, 20, 21; profound sleep 4–5
sleeping-dreaming 17
Socrates 20, 21, 46
"Something Wrong" (Eigen) 3, 67–75
soul-murder 76–77
soul-to-soul transmission 47
spirituality 45
Statman, Andy 76
"A Street Car Named Desire" (Williams) 37
Susan 75
Swenson, Karen 67
symmetrical thinking 54–55
symmetrical unconscious 56, 62, 64

temperaments, typologies of 67
texting 16
therapy interaction 12
thinking 43, 50, 52; forms of 54–55; of free association 59
time: as object for support 2; in therapy 8

timelessness 1, 3; of infinite psyche 1–2
tolerance 58, 61
Torah (Bible) 42, 44, 64
totalizing-totalitarian attitude 84
Toxic Nourishment (Eigen) 32
Tractatus (Wittgenstein) 87
Transtromer, Tomas 3
trauma, sense of 26
Tree of Knowledge 22, 42
truth 20–21; real lies off as 70

Ulysses (Joyce) 41
unconscious processes 13, 15, 37
United Nations 83
unknown emotional reality 48–49
unknown ultimate reality 43, 49

vast unconscious 16, 17
violence 36; in childhood 73; emotional 73
Vital, Chaim 47

water imagery, cross of 62–63
Whitman, Walt 14
Wiener, Jack 6
Williams, Tennessee: "A Street Car Named Desire" 37
Winnicott, D. W. 2, 15, 60, 67, 69, 79
Wittgenstein, Ludwig: *Tractatus* 87
words: inspiration 6; work with consciousness 16
Wordsworth, William: "intimations of immortality" 55

Yom Kippur 6
Yosemite God 4, 9
Yosemite Park 4

Zen Buddhism 63
Zen master 43
Zohar 43, 44, 46, 47